Heritage or Heresy

CARIBBEAN ARCHAEOLOGY AND ETHNOHISTORY

L. Antonio Curet, Series Editor

Heritage or Heresy

Archaeology and Culture on the Maya Riviera

Cameron Jean Walker

THE UNIVERSITY OF ALABAMA PRESS

Tuscaloosa

Typeface: AGaramond

∞

The paper on which this book is printed meets the minimum requirements of American National Standard for Information Sciences-Permanence of Paper for Printed Library Materials, ANSI Z39.48-1984.

Library of Congress Cataloging-in-Publication Data

Walker, Cameron Jean.
    Heritage or heresy : archaeology and culture on the Maya Riviera / Cameron Jean Walker.
        p. cm. — (Caribbean archaeology and ethnohistory)
    Includes bibliographical references and index.
    ISBN 978-0-8173-1635-8 (cloth : alk. paper) — ISBN 978-0-8173-5514-2 (pbk. : alk. paper) — ISBN 978-0-8173-8116-5 (electronic : alk. paper) 1. Mayas—Mexico—Quintana Roo (State)—Antiquities. 2. Heritage tourism—Mexico—Quintana Roo (State) 3. Culture and tourism—Mexico—Quintana Roo (State) 4. Cultural property—Mexico—Quintana Roo (State) 5. Archaeology and history—Mexico—Quintana Roo (State) 6. Archaeology and state—Mexico—Quintana Roo (State) 7. Quintana Roo (Mexico : State)—Description and travel. 8. Quintana Roo (Mexico : State)—Antiquities. I. Title.
    F1435.1.Q78W35   2009
    306.4′819097267—dc22

                                                                    2008022108

Contents

Illustrations

Heritage or Heresy

Introduction

As yet another hurricane season threatens the Caribbean, speculation turns to the potential for damage to the eastern coast of the Yucatán Peninsula, especially the city of Cancún and the Caribbean coast, popularly known as the Maya Riviera. Most of the discussion is about how the tourism industry will be affected, but there is also occasional mention of concern for the residents and an already precarious ecological system. Rarely, if ever, does the talk get around to the potential damage to the region's ancient Maya archaeological sites, although as an archaeologist, that is where my own mind veers, alongside worries for my colleagues who live there.

Along the Maya Riviera, these musings mirror the relative value accorded to tourists, locals, environment, and, finally, archaeological heritage. No one doubts that serious damage to the irreplaceable natural and cultural resources also damages the tourism industry and the local economy. They are inextricably linked in so many ways that it begs the question as to why they are ranked so low on a scale of relative social value. Is it possible that we are too quick to see the interests of tourists, locals, the environment, and the archaeological heritage as separate and distinct things?

There are at least a few lessons about the potential threat to the Maya Riviera to be learned from the damage inflicted by Hurricane Katrina on the rich heritage of New Orleans, much of which must now be rebuilt from the ground up. According to local wisdom, water flows away from the rich in New Orleans, and the greatest losses were indeed suffered by the city's poorest neighborhoods. When the city was originally founded on land that lay below sea level, there were questionable priorities and there are questionable priorities today as New Orleans struggles to gain momentum in the rebuilding process. From the very beginning, deals were made about how the land was to be developed, without much concern for the risk of hurricanes or flooding. As the city grew, deals were made for future development by filling in the wetlands that had once absorbed so much of the annual floodwater. New Orleans has now become a cautionary tale with many lessons about recognizing the potential for disaster when too many people live in a marginal landscape, how the rich are treated compared to the poor in times of crisis, and what is expedient now, as opposed to what is best for a region over the long term.

"It's not only about the tourism," complained a New Orleans resident during an interview about rebuilding, which begs the question: Are tourists valued more than residents in New Orleans? Just what are the relative values accorded to the residents, visitors, ecosystem, and heritage in New Orleans? I would argue that their values are placed in the same hierarchical order as they are in the Maya Riviera, with the potential for a similar outcome. Is the Maya Riviera yet another region poised on a knife edge?

Because the Maya Riviera is an entirely modern invention that is less than 40 years in the making, the dynamic interplay among economics, politics, demographics, and heritage makes fertile ground for anthropological inquiry. For my research, I initially planned to explore the Maya Rivera's archaeological and heritage management within the framework of a tourism-driven economy and do a focused study on how regional archaeological sites are being presented to the public. Very early on, however, it was apparent that such a narrow academic approach was inadequate because this region is not only about the tourists. It is also about the extremely poor indigenous residents, the heritage sites that also function as popular tourism destinations, and the very precarious environment that is challenged to support the rapid development and population growth.

Over time, I came to realize that even the public education question could not be explored effectively in isolation. Educating the public about archaeological sites is only a small part of a number of resources that have been tapped by the tourism industry. The public interpretation of archaeology in Quintana Roo more properly represents a symbol (or a symptom) of questionable deals made over the years, especially where human rights and environmental resources are concerned.

The Maya Riviera's sanitized resorts have now effectively erased most of the previous cultural markers and replaced them with an implausibly generic tourist destination. Scratch the carefully burnished veneer and you will find the dark underbelly formed out of greed, neglect, antipathy, and carelessness. The descendants of those who built the abandoned cities now visited by tourists are the local Maya who live in poverty in the midst of all that carefully contrived luxury. The daily crowds at some archaeological sites, particularly at Tulum, are threatening their very survival, and the delicate environmental balance is being pushed to the precipice. How could I concentrate on such a tightly defined topic when there is an 800-pound gorilla in the room? It became clear that I could not carry on as if my detached academic questions were more important than (and separate from) the region's social, economic, and environmental woes. And so, gradually, my research began to assume applied dimensions.

Public Interest in Archaeology

Public interpretation is a descriptive term used in archaeology and other disciplines to describe the official (and unofficial) versions presented at an archaeological/ heritage site or museum exhibit. Currently, television programs, movies, video games, and the popular press are the primary sources for stories about archaeology and heritage. More often than not, these stories become sensationalized in ways that no longer accurately reflect the scientific and humanistic goals of archaeological research. It is the media that currently defines archaeology to the public, but wouldn't it be better for all if the public learned about archaeological work from the archaeologists themselves rather than from other disingenuous, blatantly commercial, interests (Kwas 2000; McManamon 2000b; Paynton 2002)? At least a few scholars have recognized the need for balancing their excavation and conservation work with appropriate educational and aesthetic presentations to a visiting public. Archaeologists really need the financial and political support of the public to ensure that their research, conservation, and education efforts are able to continue, and good public education is the best way to achieve that support.

That the public holds a deep and abiding interest in archaeology is undeniable from the frequent articles in magazines and television documentaries. However, previous research on public interpretation has taught us that people are more likely to support what they understand; therefore archaeologists need to make their work intellectually, socially, and physically accessible to visitors (Davis 1997:85; Vergano 2001) (Figure 1). In essence, successful interpretation means giving archaeological information in an accurate, concise, and entertaining manner, but it also means showing the public that archaeology can be both fun and relevant in today's world (Jameson 1997:13). Without appropriate interpretation at sites, tourists often misunderstand what they see and frequently mistake restored ruins for buildings that have been left in their natural state, whereas unexcavated mounds may be mistaken for natural features of the landscape or as rubble from previous excavations (Greenwood 1989:171–185; Castaneda 1996:104) (Figure 2).

Educating tourists about the host culture not only enhances the tourist experience but is more likely to encourage behaviors that promote sustainability. For example, proper interpretive techniques can redistribute visitors in a way that relieves pressure on a particularly popular location, and important educational tools include the basics such as the presence of maps, signs, brochures, and guided tours. During my visits to the archaeological parks in Quintana Roo, I sought out the basics in interpretation, looked for innovations or anything that was distinctive, and tried to see the sites through the eyes of a tourist.

My research began with an extensive literature review on tourism (heritage and archaeological tourism in particular) for insight into the current theories and research on the subject. I found that tourism research is a relatively young field, having gained momentum only since the early 1980s, and this probably accounts for some of the more common misconceptions, especially that it is not a viable subject for scholarship. I also investigated Mexico's history of dealing with heritage and tourism issues at both the national and local levels to better understand what has led up to the current state of affairs in the Maya Riviera.

Figure 1. Tulum Archaeological Park

The public interpretation of archaeology and culture remained central to my research, as did issues surrounding cultural identity and cultural patrimony, which I
explored as part of Mexico's long emphasis on nationalism. For insight into the perspectives of locals, my research incorporated ethnographic techniques including
key informants and numerous in-depth interviews with a variety of locals, such as
Maya residents, social and environmental activists, tourism officials, and anthropologists and archaeologists at work in the region. An especially intriguing theme
that consistently emerged during those interviews was that people are quick to link
their own fate to the fate of archaeological sites in the region. It seems to me, this
sense of connection is an untapped asset that could be employed for finding effective solutions to some of the region's problems.

Several archaeological sites located in the Maya Riviera are literally inundated
with tourists on a daily basis, and their situations illustrate one of the most fundamental problems: increased tourism also accelerates deterioration. On the other
hand, if there is a strong visitor interest, it establishes that the region's heritage cap-
tures the public imagination and can help to motivate policies that would protect
that heritage from many kinds of damage.

The rewards of tourism include the potential for improved cultural understanding, but without doubt the most tangible benefits are economic. As a special
niche in the tourism industry, heritage and archaeological tourism has become a
particularly prominent strategy in Mexico, as it has in numerous other developing
nations. Economic data provide a key perspective for understanding tourism, but

Figure 2. Unexcavated mound at T'isil, Quintana Roo

other forces are also important, especially for learning more about people, their relationships, and the processes underlying culture change.

There are so many critical issues involved with the development of the Maya Riviera that it seems virtually impossible to study a single problem as separate from the rest; therefore the topic of public interpretation of archaeology became only one of several other meaningful areas of study. The continued economic exploitation of the archaeological heritage, the dire poverty of the indigenous Maya, and the spectacular but fragile landscape are inextricably linked and must be considered together.

According to Peter M. Burns (1999:71–73), both anthropology and tourism involve human and cultural dynamics, and clearly tourism is an agent of culture change. Erve Chambers (1997:3–7) has expressed the view that tourism offers an unrivaled opportunity for studying cultural processes whenever groups attempt to reconcile their differences. Clearly, the best opportunity for understanding the relationships between tourism, the environment, and the local communities lies in detailed and descriptive regional studies, so my research in the Maya Riviera has embodied a number of the relevant issues engaging modern anthropological research. The Maya Riviera provides an ideal milieu for exploring the complex state of affairs underlying tourism, with public interpretation now only one of several subtexts.

By using the Maya Riviera as a case study, this book addresses a particularly important question: how does tourism change the region? As it turns out, the question became far more interesting than the question of effective public interpretation, most obviously because there is so little thought given to public interpretation at regional archaeological sites and museums.

Taking into account the numerous definitions of tourism to have emerged over the years, my preference is for Valene Smith's version (2001:17), which says all forms of tourism require three essential elements and can be expressed as an equation: tourism = leisure time + discretionary income + positive social sanctions. This definition has the advantage in that it avoids the value judgments inherent in many other explanations for why people travel, and it provides a more neutral basis for understanding the motivations and choices of tourists.

The anthropological study of tourism provides a model for understanding many aspects of political economy, social change, natural resource management, and cultural identity. Since tourism occurs in most if not all human societies, it exerts a tremendous influence on society and the economy, making it highly relevant for anthropological study.

At its most basic level, heritage tourism is a form of economic development, and archaeologists would do well to see the tourism industry as a potential partner in raising public awareness about archaeological matters (Lynott and Wylie 2000; Slick 2002:219). The management of archaeological parks presents many challenges, but the greatest may be in keeping the resources from being destroyed by inappropriate development. Rapid changes to the region have resulted in serious environmental and social problems, which have the potential to drive away tourists and threaten the economic and social welfare of everyone who lives there.

In this book I attempt to highlight not only some of the more pressing problems by looking at the history of development in the Maya Riviera, but also the impetus for social change, and the effects at the ground level. In the end, there are even a few suggestions for the reader who might want to help take the future in hand.

1 The Public Interpretation of Archaeological Sites

The most successful interpretive strategies introduce visitors to a greater appreciation for an archaeological site and its surrounding environment. Nevertheless, archaeologists have only recently begun to focus attention on how to effectively educate visitors about their excavation and research. Interpretation and research reports were written for the benefit of funding agencies and academic peers rather than for the public. Perhaps it was felt that the public was not interested or that the subject matter was too complex, but archaeologists have been slow out of the gate to promote their work to the public. As we have learned from the case of Mexico, a nationalist ideology can not only shape how archaeology is practiced but also prompt the invention of a national archaeological past. This chapter highlights how a nation's history and contemporary politics are often crucial for determining public education policies for archaeological parks and museums (Oyuela-Caycedo 1994:5).

As suggested by noted archaeologist William Lipe (1984), there are four basic values underlying the interpretation of archaeological sites and other cultural resources. Economic value is usually the first to be considered, since archaeological/cultural resources so often come to be seen as commodities when they are opened for tourism. Second, some cultural resources may be valued for important historical associations or because they demonstrate an important architectural style or cultural tradition. Third, cultural resources have an informational value for scientific research, while the fourth, aesthetic value, comes from the often-spectacular art and architecture.

How we commemorate archaeological sites reflects the value we place on them, argue Donald Hardesty and Barbara Little (2000:5–6), although few have been fully interpreted for the public (which speaks to our priorities in the United States as well). If the acknowledged goal of public interpretation is to gain public support for research and protect the archaeological record, it is hard to explain why it is so rarely given the attention that it deserves.

An archaeological park, which is an archaeological site that has been developed for tourism, becomes a sort of outdoor museum. Often there is a sense of relaxed adventure about exploring a new area, which is usually outdoors, that even further enhances the appeal of archaeological sites (Frost 2000; Kwas 2000:341; Potter 1997; Potter and Chabot 1997; Thomas 1996).

Figure 3. Ceremonial plaza at Calakmul

Public Interpretation in Mexico

Mexico's policies for preparing archaeological sites for tourism has meant that only certain parts of the site are cleared of vegetation, leaving minimal evidence for excavation or building reconstruction. Only certain parts of a site are made accessible to the public in order to reduce maintenance costs, and unexcavated structures are considered safer when they are left under centuries of accumulated soil and vegetation. Typical of this trend are the Maya archaeological sites of Cobá and Calakmul in the Yucatán Peninsula, which are large and spread-out sites that combine a few excavated and consolidated buildings with numerous other unexcavated mounds around them. Cobá and Calakmul could be contrasted with the heavily visited sites of Chichén Itzá and Tulum, which have the vegetation almost completely cleared away in the tourist areas (Taube 2001) (Figure 3, Figure 4).

Conventional wisdom suggests that the ancient Maya ceremonial centers were kept clear of almost all vegetation, and the exposed buildings were maintained by the annual reapplication of limestone plaster and paint. As the forest took over the sites, it may have inadvertently helped to protect the buildings, while the current practice of clearing away the vegetation risks exposing the structures to even more rapid decay (Fedick 2001; Ford 1999).

Figure 4. Ceremonial plaza at Chichén Itzá

The archaeological sites discussed in this book were chosen because they are national archaeological parks located within the state of Quintana Roo. They mostly
date to the Maya Late Postclassic period with a few exceptions, but their greatest
distinction may be in their relative levels of accessibility and whether they have
made it into the guidebooks and the tourist psyche. Each site was explored for official public interpretation techniques such as signs, maps, guides, and pamphlets,
but I was also on the lookout for unofficial and alternative interpretive strategies.

Muyil, Quintana Roo

Muyil is sandwiched between the archaeological site of Tulum and the Sian Ka'an
Biosphere Reserve, a UNESCO World Heritage Site and an important ecotourism attraction. The Sian Ka'an Biosphere Reserve is similar to the national park
system in the United States, although the land is not entirely federally owned, as
with our national forests (Harris 1999:177–178; see also Simonian 1979; Batisse
1982; Gregg and McGean 1985; Halffter 1980; and Kaus 1992).

Muyil has been open for tourism since it was first excavated in the late 1980s,
but it gets minimal attention in guidebooks. To make it ready for tourism, a few
archaeological buildings were reconstituted, a few signs were added, and a nature
trail was created, but still there is little to attract visitors off the main road.

As at other Mexican archaeological parks, most of the Instituto Nacional de
Anthropologia y Historia's (INAH) signs give identical explanations in Spanish,

English, and the local Mayan language. The largest building, El Castillo, is distinguished by the carvings of two birds within a niche near the top of the pyramid, although there is only one small sign (in Spanish) with a drawing of the two birds at the front right-hand perimeter of the pyramid. Several of the other buildings have been repaired over the last several years, with thatched roofs placed over particularly vulnerable areas to offer better protection from rain and sun.

During my last visit, an INAH guard spent more time trying to book a tour to the Sian Ka'an Biosphere Reserve than in explaining the site to me. At $30 per person, he takes tourists by boat to see the spectacular water birds and a Maya ruin called the Plataforma Meditación (Meditation Platform).

The Chunyaxché ejido, which is a part of one of the largest ejidos in Mexico, sits next to Muyil, and this small community considers the park an important extension of their natural resources. However, unless they can find work as caretakers or guards at the site, they have few other employment options available in the area. As with all other Mexican archaeological sites, Muyil is administered solely by INAH, and their provisions restrict who can work as licensed guides. To be a guide requires licensing, mandatory training classes, and other standards beyond the reach of many local Maya.

Eleven families from the Chunyaxché ejido, mostly representing two lineages, live adjacent to Muyil, and two of those nuclear families organized an ecotourism cooperative. They purchased three motorboats to take tourists on short excursions into the nearby Sian Ka'an Biosphere Reserve, for which they have obtained special permission. These families also have a small workshop for making rustic bentwood furniture, and they continue to grow maize and hunt. Another opportunity for income for these families comes from selling small ornamental plants to travelers along the highway. The Amigos de Sian Ka'an, a nonprofit support group for the Sian Ka'an Biosphere Reserve, supplies potted indigenous plants for the families to cultivate and sell as a dual strategy for providing income to the families while also helping to prevent the poaching of plants from the forest. The Amigos de Sian Ka'an also encourages production of craft items, such as embroidered shirts and blouses, which they sell on consignment in regional artisan cooperatives and export to the United States.

Although these families were officially directed by the Chunyaxché ejido to work on ecotourism as a single unit, they have split up in an unfriendly manner instead. According to my sources, this split represents an unfortunate because they would have a better chance of success had they formed a consortium, at least until they were more firmly established. Since this ejido group has made the decision to move from a self-sustaining economy into a market economy, their level of success will depend upon their ability to learn the system and invest their earnings back into their fledgling ecotourism businesses.

Figure 5. Tulum beside the Caribbean Sea

Tulum, Quintana Roo

The archaeological park of Tulum is probably the most visited archaeological park in all of Mexico, at least partially because it overlooks the spectacular turquoise Caribbean Sea along a dramatic coastline lined with sparkling white sand beaches (Figure 5). Tulum's walls extend around three sides of the city, with the coastline promontory providing the fourth boundary, making this site unusual as a walled Maya city (Pearce 1984:34). Among Tulum's distinctions is that it is one of four coastal Late Postclassic centers (the others are Xel-Há, Tancah, and Soliman), all located within a few miles of each other on the east coast of the peninsula. It is especially noteworthy that Tulum is one of only a few Maya centers known to have been occupied by Maya at the time of the Conquest (Coe 2001:160; Pearce 1984:34).

Tulum also served as an important center for the Maya opposition during the mid-nineteenth-century Caste War, which became one of the longest and most successful indigenous resistance movements in the Americas. It remained a small pueblo during most of the twentieth century with subsistence based on chicle extraction, cattle ranching, and work on coconut plantations, but since the 1970s this lifestyle has been harder to sustain due to politico-economic stresses and ecological degradation (Juárez 2002:115).

Figure 6. Tiendas at Tulum

Tulum Archaeological Park is considered to be especially at risk of irreparable degradation owing to the number of people visiting the site daily. Most visitors describe Tulum as a beautiful place that has become too crowded and too commercialized. Highway directional signs now designate the entrance to Tulum as "Subway Tulum," further highlighting the prominent, if incongruous, Subway sandwich shop that sits opposite the official entrance of the ancient Maya archaeological site. Some visitors express their disappointment upon arriving at the park to see a large shopping area situated between the parking lot and the archaeological park entrance, as well as annoyance at having to fend off the ever-present *ambulantes,* or informal commercial vendors (Figure 6).

This shopping area is actually the result of lengthy negotiations and enormous pressure to allow local residents to sell souvenirs to the park's visitors. It was also meant to deter the illegal selling of souvenirs inside the park itself, although INAH reports that this concession opportunity has not entirely eliminated the persistent attempts to sell to tourists inside the archaeological park. It turns out that more than a few of these vendors are actually well-to-do outsiders who only adopt traditional Maya dress and demeanor to conduct their commercial enterprises.

Tour bus owners operate a successful business by bringing busloads of tourists to the archaeological site daily. At some point, it is likely that these tourists will buy cold drinks and a souvenir or two before they reboard the buses to return to the large resorts around Cancún. Unfortunately for the Tulum Maya, most of the revenue also leaves the area to end up in the pockets of the tour bus and resort hotel owners.

In the meantime, Tulum receives about 8,000 visitors every day, each paying about $4 to enter. From those entrance fees, INAH must pay all employee salaries and benefits, leaving little for maintenance and repair of the archaeological buildings themselves. Funding does not allow much for supplies and personnel to maintain the structures or the vegetation, although there was a major landscape renovation in 2005, with ropes added to keep visitors on the pathways and prevent access to buildings and grassy areas. In debates about the inadequacies of the present system, many, including those who operate tourism businesses, argue that they already pay state and federal taxes, so why should they have to pay extra fees to maintain the archaeological sites? While it is true that INAH does receive some funding from entrance fees for maintenance, archaeological sites are far from being self-sustaining businesses. To the contrary, INAH argues that these entrance fees generate far too little revenue to maintain the sites adequately at the present rate of annual visitors (Robles Garcia 2002).

The Tulum Pueblo

The balance between a subsistence-based economy and a large-scale commercial enterprise has shifted with time at the Tulum Pueblo and has been accompanied by increasing inequalities among the residents. Ecological degradation began in this area in the 1930s and 1940s as programs that were intended to provide equal opportunities for indigenous groups actually promoted modernization and economic development. Unlike the state of Chiapas, where state-sponsored projects and reforms may have helped to unify the indigenous populations, state intervention in Quintana Roo seems to have made conditions harder for the Maya citizens (Juárez 2002:115–116). Since the Tulum Maya already had ownership over communal lands, the ejido policy was more detrimental than helpful. At that time, the population density was much lower in Quintana Roo than in other Mexican states. For example, in 1950, Quintana Roo had 0.5 persons per square kilometer, compared to Yucatán state with 13.4 persons per square kilometer. Early on, the ejido system was fairly effective until population growth and immigration into Quintana Roo put increasing pressure on the ability of the Maya to maintain their mixed subsistence and commercial economy.

Development in the pueblo of Tulum has been very different from the towns of Pisté, Chan Kom, and Yaxley (Juárez 2002:117). Most notably, Tulum possessed qualities that were not present in these other towns, because it served simultaneously as a subsistence-level Maya village, a beachfront tourism destination, and a major archaeological tourist attraction situated on the beach.

With the onset of the tourism era, foreigners have increased the expropriation of Maya lands and resources, just as they have steadily dominated and then out-numbered the Maya population. Tulum grew from a population of 92 people in 1960 to an estimated 12,000 residents by the year 2000 (Juárez 2002:117). It is expected to grow by about 15 percent annually to reach a population of 97,000 by 2010, making it one of the fastest growing towns in Mexico.

Anthropologist Ana Juárez describes Tulum as having had a population of about 2,000 residents when she began research there in 1990, with 10 percent made up of Santa Cruz Maya (Juárez 2002:114). The rest of the immigrants were from surrounding Mexican states, having come to find work in the booming tourism economy. The second largest group was made up of Yucatec Maya, who had em-igrated from other parts of the peninsula. As these immigrants have moved into Tulum, ejido membership has doubled from about 60 in the early 1970s to about 120 in 1992, usually involving transferred property rights as families moved into the area to take advantage of the economic opportunities afforded by tourism (Juárez 2002:117–118).

Today's Tulum Maya descendants identify themselves as people of the Santa Cruz, or members of the Iglesia Maya political-ceremonial centers where the mi-raculous cross and saints are housed (Juárez 2002:113–124). The most recent groups to move into the Tulum pueblo have been foreigners, expatriates, and entrepreneurs from North America and Europe. Today, these different ethnic groups live in sepa-rate barrios and show some class differences that have become more pronounced as tourism has increased.

Ecological degradation in the region has been detailed by Ueli Hostettler (1996: 176–179) and includes a decline in game animals, particularly those considered conducive for the tourism industry. The Maya face fines or the possibility of ar-rest for harvesting their customary foodstuffs, especially turtles, turtle eggs, conch, and lobster, which also happen to be highly valued by tourists. A scarcity of poles and thatch for building traditional Maya houses and buildings has also been re-ported in this area.

Official designation of the Sian Ka'an Biosphere Reserve in 1986 made even this large tract of land off-limits to the local Maya and further limited their access to local natural resources (Juárez 2002:116). In fact, tourism development may have actually worsened the ability of the local Maya to gain sustenance from the land and has led to a gradual replacement by work for wages.

When discussing the environment, many Maya use metaphorical language, and roads provide a key cultural metaphor because they allow the incorporation of both prophetic and oral traditions. According to Juárez, the fast-changing modern world corresponds to significant prophecies of other drastic changes to come (2002:119). A number of prophecies allow the Tulum pueblo to explain the ways of the world, but one particularly intriguing prophecy foretells an end of the tourism era: "The elders foretold that fields would no longer be productive, food would be scarce, humans would lose both the desire and the ability to procreate, young children would die, people would wear gold shoes and clothes, they would be surrounded by people speaking many languages, and they would have to buy water, among many other points. While the Maya critique some contemporary changes, many understand the tremendous changes of the tourist era in the context of their prophetic tradition" (Juárez 2002:119). Such prophecies seek to address the increasingly obvious disparity between how the Maya of Tulum live and how the tourists live while staying in the upscale beachside hotels around Tulum. For these Maya, the wave of tourism is yet another kind of invasion, but this too can be endured until it ends, and then life will return to a semblance of normality.

Cobá, Quintana Roo

The ancient city of Cobá was a dominant power before the Itzá invasion and is especially notable for the numerous Maya *sacbeob*, or raised causeways, which radiate away from Cobá in all directions. The site has always held special power for the Maya and continues to draw pilgrimages today. One reason for Cobá's early and sustained significance lies with the rare grouping of five lakes nearby. By using a series of dikes and dams, the area was able to support an estimated population of 40,000–60,000 people (Coe 2001:404–405). Another aspect of Cobá's archaeological significance lies in the presence of a stela with an exceptionally early date of 3188 B.C., which has attracted the attention of Maya scholars, archaeology buffs, and New Age believers alike.

Cobá has always been considered a place with supernatural potency and is still used for local Maya ceremonies (Brown 1999:297–298). Interestingly, it is also viewed as a place that has been cursed by malevolent spirits, so it is still deemed important to burn candles at the base of the main pyramid to keep them at bay. Some informants report that if the sacrificing ceremonies are ever discontinued, the people of Cobá will soon begin to die (Figure 7).

The Carnegie Institution first excavated Cobá in the years between 1926 and 1930, and the proximity to water made it an attractive campsite for chicleros in the 1940s (Brown 1999:298). INAH's Centro Regional del Sureste began investigations there in 1974, producing a large-scale map with the help of the National Geographic Society, although mostly salvage and reconstruction work has been performed since 1984. A guard station was established at the site around this time, and a caretaker from the town of Chemax was hired to work at the site. However, as told by Denise Brown, the caretaker and his family soon left to return to Chemax because of his six-year-old daughter's unexplained illness, which they thought was brought on by living too close to Cobá's ancient buildings. According to one informant: "The powers of Cobá emanate from the ruins of a huge and beautiful city

Figure 7. La Eglesia structure, Cobá

whose ruling class became abusive and evil, thereby cursing the city and its inhabitants. According to Don Pepe Mahla of Chemax, the city will reemerge and will
be again sparkling and spectacular, because it was built by the ancient people and
had its own king. Don Pepe pointed out the splendor of Cobá was and will be far
greater than that of Cancún, which has no past or future in his view. It falls outside
of these cycles of time and events" (Brown 1999:298).

Not all archaeological sites in the region are thought to hold such strong supernatural powers, but the Maya regard Cobá and Tulum as particularly cursed and
potentially dangerous places. Also associated with Cobá and Tulum are numerous
aluxes, or figures associated with misfortunes that occur in the surrounding forests and are thought to represent ancient individuals who were transformed as a
form of punishment. Other sites not generally associated with kings were also
thought to have been cursed but have now lost their power, particularly after the
stone and clay alux figurines were removed. These sites will never again be important
settlements for the Maya. A third category of sites includes those that have never
had supernatural powers and have never been dangerous for the modern Maya.

The unobtrusive entrance to the site of Cobá is easy to miss unless the visitor
pays especially close attention. It lies at the extreme right-hand corner of a dirt
parking lot lined at either side by shops and cafes. Official INAH signs are located
just inside the entrance, although no brochures or pamphlets are available (Figure 8).

Figure 8. Entrance signs at Cobá

The grounds of Cobá Archaeological Park are extensive and heavily wooded, with most of the unexcavated structures barely perceptible amid the dense vegetation. According to one vacation website for the Maya Riviera, Cobá is "a less traveled site, the ruins aren't manicured like Chichén Itzá and Tulum and retain that jungle feel" (www.locogringo.com). Only a handful of directional signs are in place to guide the visitor through the large site, so there is little sense of context about how the buildings may have been used or may have appeared in their heyday. Several of the signs are now badly faded, as exemplified by a small, barely readable sign near a ball court that says "juego de pelota," without further explanation .

The grounds of Cobá are lush, and over the last several years most buildings have been roped off to prevent visitors from climbing on them. The Castillo and a few other buildings are still available for climbing if the intrepid explorer is able to brave the fierce tropical heat and humidity. A once intricately carved limestone stela, now badly eroded, bears a sign with a scaled line drawing but lacks any further explanation (Figure 9) (Figure 10).

The modern village of Cobá was settled about 60 years ago by Yucatec Maya agriculturalists, and Cobá has been described as a traditional Maya community in that it depends upon agriculture and adheres to the principles of reciprocity to maintain social connectedness. For subsistence purposes, each family was granted the use of about 50 hectares of land for slash-and-burn agriculture in addition to having home gardens and room for raising pigs and chickens. In many cases, how-

Figure 9. Stela at Cobá

Figure 10. Climb down El Castillo, Cobá

Figure 11. Bicycle rentals at Cobá

ever, these holdings have now been reduced to less than 20 hectares per household, and at least one-third of the men of Cobá now work outside the community rather than practice subsistence agric ulture (Pi-Sunyer, Thomas, and Daltabuit 2001:130–132).

Many villagers argue that the most promising way to earn money lies with the adjacent archaeological park. More than 70,000 tourists visit the site of Cobá annually, and they also browse the locally owned shops and cafes for cold drinks and souvenirs. It is estimated that about 40 percent of Cobá's working population earns at least some income from tourism, and the area has recently become more aggressively marketed for ecotourism excursions (Pi-Sunyer, Thomas, and Daltabuit 2001:130–132). These entrepreneurs make up a new class of merchants, shopkeepers, and restaurant owners at Cobá and further widen the differences in social status within this small community.

One particular private enterprise stands out on Cobá's large and forested grounds: it is now possible to rent mountain bicycles to ride the considerable distances between the excavated and consolidated monumental structures. The rentals are owned and operated by the local Maya and are especially popular with tourists at this site because it is so spread out in the forest (Figure 11). Although INAH officials have received some complaints about tourists riding their bicycles on the ancient structures, the local Maya have stationed a man at each of the ancient structures to keep a close eye on the visitors' activities as well as direct them to park the bikes at least 50 feet away from the buildings. Although bicycle rentals are not typically found at Mexican archaeological parks, such an enterprise is also offered by the Lacandon Maya at the site of Bonampak in the state of Chiapas.

El Rey, Quintana Roo

Located on Punta Nisuc in Cancún's Zona Turista, El Rey is the largest archaeological zone in the immediate vicinity (Figure 12). Although most of the structures date to the Late Postclassic, some think parts of the site may actually have originated in the Classic era, and the site probably served as a port for trading vessels (Coe 2001:417–418). The name El Rey refers to a small sculpture found when William Sanders first explored the site in 1954. Miguel, the elegant and knowledgeable guide who took me around the site, seemed more interested in trying to figure out what I wanted to hear rather than in answering my questions about public interpretation. His spiel is consistent with that of numerous guides and confirms the assertion that many are not averse to saying whatever will please their clients. Guides are especially prone to emphasize the more sensational aspects of Maya life, including human sacrifices and frequent warfare, as well as common misconceptions about the Maya as peaceful astronomer-kings.

Most of the tourists who visit this site come from Europe and the United States, and the guides often try to match the tone and direction of their presentations to the nationality of the tourist. According to Miguel, Europeans have a long social history that involves great kings and frequent warfare, so it is easier to begin with descriptions of kings, priests, and warrior elite. Miguel sees Europe as the Mother Culture of the West, and this view provides Europeans with insights that are not so readily apparent to Americans and Canadians. It is first necessary to explain a nondemocratic sociopolitical organization to American and Mexican tourists before launching into the archaeological descriptions, although interestingly, Miguel mentions that Cherokee Indians from the United States occasionally make special trips to El Rey to get in touch with the spirit world of the Maya.

As for making the connection with the ancient and modern Maya, Miguel claims that many guides are trained to place emphasis on this connection during their interactions with tourists. He says that some tourists, usually those already interested in the liberal arts, are the most keen to learn about the modern Maya. The Maya themselves are proud of their heritage and occasionally visit this and other sites, but El Rey is particularly accessible to Maya workers in the Cancún tourist zone. Most of the attendants who work at El Rey also speak Mayan and often

Figure 12. El Rey Archaeological Park

listen to a local radio station, Radio Turquesa, which broadcasts solely in Yucatec Mayan.

When asked about the commercial representation of the ancient and modern Maya, Miguel suggests that Xcaret's staged shows are very popular and present a fairly balanced staging of the duality (both good and bad) of the ancient and the modern Maya. To be successful, Miguel suggests, a guide must be intuitive and follow conversational leads in order to deliver the level of information that will satisfy the visitor's interests.

Miguel says there are three different types of reasons that a tourist may express interest in visiting a site, and they stem from the belly, the heart, or the head. Those he connects to the belly are the spontaneous visitors who act and react intuitively. Those who come from the heart are usually drawn by feelings of empathy or a deeply felt connection with the past, while those whose interest stems from the head already possess a certain amount of knowledge and have a keener intellectual appreciation of the Maya. Revealingly, as we discussed the site, Miguel kept reverting to his standard "spiel" in relating astronomical and iconographic details unless he was diverted by very specific questions. This suggests to me that he was either unclear about my objectives for the visit or that I did not fit neatly into any of his three paradigms for visitors. From my perspective, I grew progressively more skeptical about the things he was telling me as he introduced some highly questionable interpretations.

As with numerous other tourist venues, this site has an appeal on a more mundane level as well: El Rey is also notable for the numerous iguanas that inhabit the site, and guides often carry small bags of bread to attract them if a visitor shows interest.

El Meco, Quintana Roo

When trying to locate the archaeological site of El Meco in Northern Cancún, there are only two small signs along the main highway entering Ciudad Cancún from the south but no signs whatsoever were seen within the city itself. After I asked for directions several times, a single sign for El Meco was spotted on the road leading out of the northern city limits of Ciudad Cancún. The few directional signs that are in place are in Spanish, and none has English or Maya translations. If a visitor actually manages to find the site, there is only one inconspicuous sign announcing the entrance to El Meco. Needless to say, there were no other tourists during my visit, and a subsequent visit found the site closed by 3:00 in the afternoon even though the entrance sign states that the park was open until 5:00 p.m. It is no wonder that the site is rarely visited, and INAH has received a number of complaints about the lack of signage for this lesser-known archaeological site.

Xel-Há, Quintana Roo

A recent advertisement explains that the ancient Maya name of *Xel-Há* translates into "where the water is born," and this area has served alternately as a pre-Hispanic trading port, a safe harbor for mariners, and a pilgrimage site. The park is now marketed as an underwater snorkeler's paradise: "Legend had it that Mayan gods combined their wisdom, dreams and love of beauty to create a place that would bring together the best of the Caribbean. They declared the iguana the land's guardian, the parrot-fish the sea's guardian, and they named their creation Xel-Há. They were so pleased with their work that they decided to share it with man" (Cancún Tips 2001b:36).

Built by the same consortium that built Xcaret Ecoarchaeological Park, Xel Há is billed as the largest natural aquarium in the world and is an ecosystem that is now shared by people in a very big way. Situated in a narrow, rocky inlet near excavated ancient ruins, it covers 10 square acres and has more than 50 species of fish and a multitude of underwater caves to explore. Brochures claim that park entrance fees support an underwater research laboratory, and it is even possible to see the ruins of submerged temples in the depths of the clear water (Pearce 1984:34).

A short distance to the south of the lagoon lie the ancient Maya ruins also called Xel-Há, but even though they are located only a few feet off the highway, tourists

Figure 13. Facilities at Xcaret Ecoarchaeological Park

rarely visit these large and fairly well-preserved ancient ruins. Clearly, the marketing strategy for the park has been to emphasize the snorkeling and commercial offerings, and the archaeological site is a secondary consideration.

Xcaret, Quintana Roo

Promoted as "Nature's Sacred Paradise," the name Xcaret is said to derive from a local corruption of the Spanish word for *caleta* or inlet. The site represents one of the larger Postclassic East Coast style ceremonial centers on Quintana Roo's coast (Kelly 1993:321). For over a thousand years, Maya pilgrims have stopped at Xcaret to purify themselves in the sacred cenote before embarking in canoes for Cozumel and the sacred shrine of the goddess Ix chel (Andrews and Andrews 1975; Kelly 1993:322).

In 1991, Xcaret became one of the most controversial scenes involving tourism development when the site was transformed into an $8.1 million "eco-archaeological" amusement park (Figure 13). A large section of the park was dynamited, bulldozed, and dredged to build two underground rivers for swimming through a series of caverns over 530 meters in length and taking about 45 minutes each to float down. The park was built on the ancient Maya port of Polé and, according to one advertisement, "was created to encourage the harmonious mingling of its visitors with Mother Earth and the cultural legacy of the Mayan world" (Cancún Tips 2001a). Visitors enter Xcaret through a replica of the arch at Labná (located in the

state of Yucatán), surrounded by a museum, restaurants, and gift shops that suggest a pyramid "designed to blend and harmonize with the natural surroundings."
There is a special inlet with fish and plants for those who want to snorkel, although
even the guidebooks note that most of the fish are now gone. The park offers an
opportunity to swim with dolphins for about $80 per person on a first-come, first-
served basis, and it also boasts botanical gardens, cenotes, a petting zoo, a small archaeological museum, restaurants, a bar, and a water-sports center.

Moreover, the park has been as controversial for the vast changes to the environment as for the subsuming of the archaeological buildings scattered throughout
the grounds of Xcaret. Visitors to Xcaret are able to explore the ancient ruins situated throughout the site, although the buildings are poorly marked on maps and
signage. In fact, visitors who only want to see the ancient Maya buildings are asked
to pay the park's steep entrance fee (about $45), although there is an agreement
with INAH that a visitor can visit the archaeological ruins by paying the standard
INAH fee of about $4.00. When we asked about this option at the ticket booth,
we were told that this is not always possible and must be arranged in advance to allow a special escort to the area.

This type of limited access to the archaeological site goes against the spirit of
Mexican laws on cultural patrimony and public access to Mexico's cultural heritage.
In the unlikely event that INAH were to attempt to expropriate the site from pri-
vate management, Xcaret's owners maintain the legal option of deciding whether
or not to sell, and such a controversial move would have reverberations throughout
Mexico.

INAH has claimed that they are supposed to receive an annual payment in lieu
of specific gate receipts; however, no payment has been recorded since the park
opened in 1991. Local press coverage of this dispute between INAH and Xcaret
emphasizes the concerns of local ecologists, who continue to decry the damage
done by construction and by the heavy flow of visitors. INAH has been criticized
for making concession deals with the owners of Xcaret, leading to further ani-
mosity between INAH and the owners, who in turn make declarations to the press
that they have already paid the disputed funds to INAH.

On August 1, 2002, Centro INAH officials issued a statement to the press titled
"El INAH No Ha Recibido Ninguna Solicitud Para Realizar Obra Por Parte de la
Empreza Xcaret":

En referencia a diversas notas periododisticas publicadas en días pasados, con
relación a la situacion de la zona arqueológica de Xcaret, Quintana Roo, el
Instituto Antropología e Historía informa:

• El INAH no ha otorgado ninguna concesión a la Promotora Xcaret, para
explotar comercialmente la zona arqueológia del mismo nombre.

- Desde 1986 el INAH ha realizado trabajos de investigación y conservación arqueológica en la zona de Xcaret. Debido a la gran cantidad de visitants que recibe el lugar, ha sido necesario que este Instituto intnesifique las acciones de mantenimeinto y restauración, que han significado un esguerzo adicional para su conservación.
- El INAH habilitó desde 1995 el acceso a la zona arqueológica de Xcaret, en el cual, el boloto do entrada tiene un costa de $27.00 (veintisiete pesos) por persona, como en muchos otros sitias del país, conforme a lo establacido en la Ley Federal de Derechos. Este acceso de independiento del correspondiento al Parque Xcaret, manejado por la promotora del mismo nombre.
- En cuanto a la supuesta realización de nuevas obras dentro del area de la polygonal de la zona de monumentos arqueológicos, el INAH no ha recibido ninguna solicitud por parte de la Promocion a Xcaret. Ni se ha presentado ningún proyecto hast el momento a fin de valorarlo.
- Las decisions del Instituto Nacional de Antropolgía e Historía con relación a la zona arqueológica de Xcaret, se han tomado y tomarán con estricto apego a la Ley Federal sobre Monumentos y Zonas Arqueológicos, Artisticos e Históricos.

El INAH reitera su postura de proteger, en el marco de sus atribuciones legales, el patrimonio cultural de los mexicanos.

The English translation reads as follows: "INAH has not received any work solicitation from Xcaret."

As it relates to the newspaper articles recently published about the Xcaret archaeological zone in Quintana Roo, the Institute of Anthropology and History informs:

- INAH has not given any concessions to "Promotora Xcaret" to commercially exploit the Xcaret archeological zone.
- Since 1986, INAH has been doing research and preservation works in the Xcaret archeological zone. Due to the heavy traffic of visitors, the institute has put forth additional efforts in the restoration and preservation works of the zone.
- Since 1995, INAH has allowed public access to the zone. The entrance ticket costs 27 pesos per person, which is similar to many other sites in the country, and in accordance with the Federal Law of Rights (Ley Federal de Derechos). "Promotora Xcaret" handles the access to the park.

- The INAH does not have any proposals from "Promotora Xcaret" regarding the supposedly new works in the zone of the archeological monuments. At the moment, no project has been presented for evaluation.   .
- All the decisions related to the Xcaret archeological zone have been and will continue to be made by INAH, in strict compliance with the Federal Law for Monuments and Archeological Zones, Artistic, and Historical Sites.

The INAH reiterates its position to protect within its legal attributions, the cultural patrimony of the Mexicans.

For all intents and purposes, the ruins at Xcaret are presented as yet another source of amusement for park visitors, and there is little to protect the buildings from being damaged by the large crowds.

Xcaret's parking lot is said to accommodate approximately 7,000 visitors, in addition to the crowds brought in by the brightly painted pink-and-blue Xcaret buses. They also come on day trips from Cancún and the other resorts along the coast to enjoy picnics in areas filled with hammocks and *palapas* for shade, changing rooms with lockers, bathrooms, and showers, not to mention restaurants, ice cream vendors and other concessions.

"Xcaret Nights" is a professionally staged and orchestrated sound-and-light show in a new and well-designed auditorium that is partially roofed but open to the air at window levels. As visitors proceed along the walkway toward the arena, they are presented with elaborately conceived tableaux of actors wearing elaborately detailed costumes and playing instruments made of conch and turtle shells. As visitors enter the amphitheater-style auditorium, they are handed small-skirted candles before being seated on smooth limestone tiered benches padded with plastic cushions. Actors dressed in indigenous costumes mount the highest reaches of the auditorium to announce the start of the show by blowing into enormous conch shells. With this cue, dozens of costumed dancers parade onto the stage floor to elaborately choreographed music (Figure 14).

The first act consists of a reenactment of the Maya ball game as played on a basketball-sized court with the players dressed in breechcloths and elaborate headdresses. As the game progresses, the actors/ballplayers begin to incorporate the steeply sloped walls in their efforts to direct the ball through the single hoop mounted in the top-center portion in each of the two walls. There is accompanying music and narration in the Yucatec Mayan language as the game is played.

After the ball game, there is a staged reenactment of a New Fire ceremony, performed without verbal explanation and with an actor walking on stilts to portray an old man with a basket of fire on his back. After he gives the fire to the ballplay-

Figure 14. Beginning of program at Xcaret with actors dressed in costume

ers, the ball game is again played with the ballplayers dressed more formally in white smocks and headbands, but this time the ball is dramatically on fire.

After an intermission opportunity to purchase food and drinks and light the skirted candles, and again without explanation, there is an announcement to observe a moment of silence "to honor our rich cultural heritage."

One of the most intriguing performances involved a reenactment of the "first contact" between the Spanish conquistadors and Mexican indigenous peoples. As the Spaniards emerged from the right side of the stage, the crowd spontaneously booed loudly, while they cheered when the indigenous peoples emerged from the opposite side of the stage. There was a choreographed symbolic meeting, with the two groups warily circling each other in the center of the stage until a stylized battle began. The Spaniards steadily advanced on the Indians until they edged them off-stage, and at this point, the conquistadors rode horses across the stage, followed by priests carrying a burning cross, which was then erected at one corner of the stage. This was the climax to the evening's performance and was followed by yet another moment of silence abruptly broken by loud, upbeat Mexican music and a parade of costumed dancers performing various traditional Mexican dances.

Ironically, this public display of indigenous ceremonies and dances may be in violation of Mexican law, which forbids reproducing Maya rituals and dances. It is equally ironic that these dances and ceremonies are actually Aztec dances since there are no known records that describe ancient Maya dancing.

The success of Xcaret's public interpretation of archaeology and culture is demonstrated by statistics indicating that more than one-third of all the tourists who come to Cancún also visit Xcaret. This amounts to more than 40,000 visitors each month and makes Xcaret's audiences some of the largest audiences for "staged productions" in all of Mexico (Travel Channel 2003).

The Basics of Interpretation

INAH archaeologist Alejandro Muriel has done research to suggest that a site visit is most successful when there is architectural variety and a sense of urban design and when several different periods of occupation are adequately highlighted. A visit also needs to be supported by appropriate signage and a printed guidebook: "Proper preparation of a site for visitors is like writing a book with illustrations at a scale of 1:1" (Muriel 2001:59). INAH's main strategy has been to place signs with identical descriptions in Spanish, English, and the regional indigenous language at the entrance and at a few particularly noteworthy locations around a site.

For the time being, Mexican policy concedes that the best way to learn about a site is to hire a professional guide. This strategy offers employment opportunities for qualified locals and gives them a stake in providing a successful visitor experience, especially since guides rely heavily on tips. Even though the quality of information provided by local guides is often open to question, INAH licensing requires taking annual classes to learn about the latest findings. On the other hand, it comes down to what pleases the public and there is very little to prevent guides from saying whatever their audiences will believe. Selling brochures and maps at each site would augment other attempts at public education and could be a potential funding source, but at this point the infrastructure does not appear to be able to produce explanatory literature on a continual basis (Figure 15, Figure 16).

Even though the solutions to problems of managing heritage sites often seem to be as complicated as the problems themselves, archaeologists need to be at the forefront of the decision-making process when archaeological sites are opened for archaeology. In the United States, cultural property laws have generally followed on the heels of environmental laws, but effective policies are not enough in and of themselves, given that policies also require prompt and appropriate enforcement.

Since proactive measures require extra funding, local and federal governments usually rank archaeology as a low priority when compared with other more pressing cultural and environmental concerns. However, officials occasionally come to realize the political and financial potential that comes with the public's interest in tourism, and this gives hope that at least some of the revenue will eventually be directed to public education.

Some Mexican states have pitched in with federal INAH funds in order to build quality museums near their archaeological sites. The state of Chiapas has not only been able to maintain the lush grounds at Palenque and Yaxchilán but has also built impressive local museums near the entrance to Palenque's archaeological park and

Figure 15. Guide with tourists at Cobá

Figure 16. Licensed tour guide in action

in the ejido Frontera Corazol, near the site of Yaxchilán. Similarly, the state of Yucatán helped to build the innovative museum at the archaeological site of Dzibilchaltun, just outside the city of Mérida.

Pseudoarchaeology and Interpretation

Pseudoarchaeology books and television shows are extremely popular and provide the public with information (more often misinformation) about archaeological sites. It is frustrating to realize that these spokesmen have such access to publicity and funding, while dedicated archaeologists struggle usually without much of either. Clearly, archaeologists are not very good at selling their work to the public, even though they have plenty of great stories for the telling. Archaeologists must learn to tap into that reservoir of public interest in order to define their discipline and make their issues understandable and relevant. To those who would argue that these kinds of popular documentaries actually create public interest in the subject, a marine archaeologist, Nicholas Flemming, replied, "It is a bit like committing a murder because that gets justice talked about. There are other ways to the same end" (Fagan 2003:49).

An even bigger problem may be that only a handful of archaeologists actually recognize the need to share their findings with the public, preferring instead to disseminate information among their peers and students. Even when archaeologists are aware of the need to provide educational and interpretive information, doing so takes a different skill set and is hard to do well. Most archaeologists are less than effective storytellers, probably because archaeological training has emphasized a discursive rather than a narrative communication format (Kennedy 2002:xiii; Young 2002:241).

Awareness that public interpretation is a crucial professional obligation has been growing, although only a handful of American universities have incorporated public education into their curriculum. Even so, some of the leading voices on public interpretation are in the United States, particularly in the National Park Service and the Bureau of Land Management, and the two largest professional organizations, the Society for American Archaeology and the Archaeological Institute of America, maintain active public education committes.

Interestingly, Mayanists as a subgroup of archaeologists represent a notable exception to this academic bias because they have long made their scholarship available to a popular audience. Karl Taube (1993) and Michael Coe (1993) are among the more prominent academicians who have written popular books, appeared in television documentaries, and led public tours to Maya archaeological sites to oblige the enormous public interest in ancient Mesoamerica (McManamon 2000a).

2 A Brief History of Mexican Archaeology

The tradition of Mexican archaeology dates back to at least 1776, when an *instrucción* of the Royal Cabinet of Natural History was established to excavate antiquities for royal collections. Military men and bureaucrats were among the first national archaeologists when the Mexican National Antiquities Council (Junta de Antiguedades) was formed in 1822. The first Inspector of Archaeological Monuments was established in 1885 with Leopoldo Batres, an amateur archaeologist, serving in the position. Captain Porfírio Díaz, Jr., the son of then-President Porfírio Díaz, was so interested in archaeology that he served as an assistant to Batres during the rescue operation of the Aztec Templo Mayor in Mexico City in 1901 (Litvak 1985).

Having established an early historical precedent, the support of Mexican archaeological projects has since meant currying favor with current government executives. Batres established the first official archaeological zones, most notably Teotihuacán, Mitla, Xochicalco, and Monte Albán, which were essentially open-air museums for educating the public about the pre-Hispanic origins of the Mexican people. By 1912, the general inspector had two subinspectors situated in the states of Yucatán and Chiapas, and by 1994 there were 157 explored and partially restored archaeological zones set up throughout the nation.

The development of the Mexican School of Archaeology in the years between 1917 and the 1950s has occasionally been characterized as the "golden period," beginning with the tenures of Manuel Gamio and José Reygadas Vertiz. An exciting and productive blend of archaeological and anthropological theories emerged that incorporated scientific applications with an emphasis on the reconstruction of certain monumental architecture (Robles Garcia 2002:chap. 2). The Mexican School of Archaeology has always placed great emphasis on the four-field approach, offering training in physical anthropology, ethnology, linguistics, and archaeology as early as 1906 (Avila 1995:312; Robles Garcia 2002). Also during this time, other important personages, including Franz Boas, Alfred Tozzer, and Eduardo Seler, founded the International School of Archaeology and American Ethnography, with support from Mexico, the United States, and several European countries.

Manuel Gamio, Mexico's first professionally trained archaeologist, was strongly influenced by Franz Boas, particularly in incorporating the interdisciplinary applications of scientific methodologies as a way to study human history. By most accounts, Gamio was an able administrator who served in many politically appointed positions, most notably as director of anthropology under the Secretary of Agriculture and Development in 1917, and as Undersecretary of Public Education in 1924 (Robles Garcia 2002:chap. 2). Employing governmental policy and financial support, the Mexican School institutionalized archaeology programs for training, research, and reconstructed some of the more spectacular monuments. Public education about archaeology was also embraced as a means to encourage a sense of pride in national identity (Schavelzon 1981; Villalpando 2001).

Gamio has been credited with developing the concept of a practical (some might say political) motivation for scientific archaeology by declaring that research had both an archaeological component and a "patriotic instruction" component (Gamio 1960; León 1994:80). Later, to escape charges of political corruption, Gamio was forced to flee to the United States, where he then turned his attention to social anthropology and the *indigenista* sociopolitical movement (León 1994:78–83).

Gamio's successor, Alfonso Caso, successfully merged the interests of archeology with education-in-the-government interest by boosting archaeology to a status profession. Caso became the first general director of INAH in 1939, and his earlier experience as a politician facilitated the synthesis of the two traditions of governmental archaeology and museums. Caso had two lifelong projects: the excavation and reconstruction of Monte Albán and gaining a greater understanding of tourism's impact on the monuments. A lawyer by training, Caso also worked to instill a legal basis for archaeological research, and in 1939, Mexican law declared that all archaeological monuments were public property to be managed by the federal government (Robles Garcia 2002:chap. 2).

Mexican officials quickly recognized that the spectacular archaeological discoveries provided equally grand opportunities for tourism promotion. The budding concept of nationalism helped to make archaeology a centerpiece of the national consciousness, and the Mexican government began tourism promotion in earnest at the same time.

The Development of INAH

Within INAH, two entities govern archaeological research. The first is the Coordinacíon Nacional de Arqueologia (National Coordination of Archaeology), which plans, sets priorities, and coordinates activities to achieve specified objectives and supports the departments charged with the preservation of cultural heritage. The coordinacíon also administers the Departments of Research and Conservation, Archaeological Salvage, Public Registry of Archaeological Zones, Planning and Evaluation, and Laboratories and Academic Support. These departments work with the various sections of INAH archaeological centers in different parts of the country and with the Technical Archive to maintain all written and graphical information produced by the research.

The second entity, Consejo de Arqueologia (Council of Archaeology), is a collegial committee made up of representatives from different Mexican institutions working on archaeological projects, in conjunction with the researchers and administrators from INAH. The consejo analyzes and evaluates proposals for all archaeological research to be done within Mexican territory and in national waters. Responsibilities range from the initial presentation of research proposals to the submission of final reports, including all of the physical materials recovered, according to the standards set by the Disposiciones Reglamentarias para la Investigacion Arqueological en Mexico (Rules for the Disposition of the Archaeological Investigations in Mexico).

According to Muriel (2001:56–57), between 200,000 and 250,000 known archaeological sites are distributed throughout the territories of Mexico, ranging from temporary camps and caves to enormous cities like Teotihuacán. Of this vast number, more than 200 archaeological zones are presently open to the public. To manage this tremendous responsibility, INAH employs some 400 staff archaeologists and a greater number of future professionals-in-training, making it one of the largest employers of archaeologists in the world.

Although these figures do not include archaeological salvage projects or registered archaeological sites, by 1996, INAH had carried out more than 200 projects, of which 58 were sites open to public. Another 47 projects were carried out by other Mexican or foreign institutions, with 11 of the 1995 projects situated at sites that were open to the public (Muriel 2001:57).

A tradition of restorer-archaeologist training also emerged, involving such personages as Alfonso Caso, Jorge Acosta, Ignacio Bernal, Miguel Angel Fernández, Manuel Gamio, Ignacio Marquina, José Reygadas, and Alberto Ruiz working alongside several foreign institutions (Muriel 2001:57). Sylvanus Morley, with the Carnegie Institution of Washington, performed much of the restoration work that can be seen today at Chichén Itzá, helping to launch a period when most of the archaeological work was concentrated on the great archaeological centers of Teotihuacán, Monte Albán, Palenque, and Chichén Itzá.

Archaeological research at these monumental sites provided a template for how the Maya and other indigenous groups were to be officially portrayed to the public. These early pioneers are now criticized for their tendency to focus their efforts on the reconstruction of the largest pyramids and temples, therefore emphasizing the Maya elite rather than the society as a whole (McClung de Tapia 2002; Muriel 2001:57). Another criticism is that among the most common restoration errors was a failure to indicate clearly the differences between the original sections of buildings and the sections that have been reconstructed, which may not be obvious to the visiting public.

The prominence of the New Archaeology movement in the 1970s brought more emphasis on incorporating science into archaeology as a new generation of

Mexican archaeologists rejected the massive reconstructions of the elite archaeological zones and focused instead on studying settlement patterns and cultural ecology (Muriel 2001:57–58). Over the next 20 years, the change in emphasis placed considerably less importance on the restorer tradition, with the unfortunate consequence of further deterioration of pre-Hispanic buildings and a shortage of trained restoration professionals (McClung de Tapia 2002).

Eventually, restoration programs and maintenance projects again gained prominence in a field that is now considered to be multidisciplinary, although there is something of a schism between the proponents for the importance of research and those who advocate for the necessity of preparing a site for public visits. Muriel (2001:58) sees the necessities of research and of public interpretation as complementary rather than oppositional, because research determines the foundation for a greater understanding about what should be presented to public. All too often, the complementarities have been hampered by the lack of a coherent set of principles for deciding important questions such as how and for whom the ruins are to be restored, which building is to be restored, and which period is to be emphasized.

The Influence of *Indigenismo* on Mexican Archaeology

The concept of *Indigenismo*, or the idealization of indigenous cultures, probably dates back to the writings of Bartolomé de las Casas. Another commonly used term, *mestizaje*, actually has two meanings: a genetic blend of European, American, and African populations and a cultural blend of indigenous and imported traditions into a synthesized Mexican culture (van den Berghe 1995:569–570). As outgrowths of the Mexican Revolution of 1910–1917, indigenismo and mestizaje officially replaced *nacionalismo* to become the principal components of Mexican nationhood (van den Berghe 1995:569).

At the time of Mexico's independence in the mid-nineteenth century, indigenous peoples were relegated to the bottom of the hierarchy, even though President Benito Juárez himself was known to have Zapotec ancestry. Mexico appeared to be moving toward a society more stratified by class than by race until after the revolution, when a new concept of indigenismo began to take shape (van den Berghe 1995:569).

As early as 1917, Manuel Gamio, as the founder of Mexican indigenism, outlined a strategy for integrating archaeological and anthropological studies at settlements around the ancient site of Teotihuacán (Gutiérrez 1999:91–93). There, Mexican anthropologists applied the concept of indigenism to address the sociocultural complexities of the multiethnic population. *Forjando patria* (forging the patriotism) was seen as a way to achieve modernity, although it remains a matter of debate as to whether Gamio actually intended to put an end to the remaining indigenous cultures.

By the 1940s, a new style of indigenism glorified the Indian past and was seen as a vindication of Indian-ness by providing the primary rationale for incorporating them into the nation-state. Indians were seen as a means to promote development by placing emphasis upon integration while maintaining respect for the unique Indian identities. Despite the fact that few if any Indians actually participated, the indigenist movement had established two primary goals: to achieve national integration and to use Indian-ness as a criterion for defining the national culture of Mexico. Mesoamerican indigenous populations were then idealized as a central component of contemporary Mexican culture, while simultaneously de-emphasizing Spanish contributions to the hybrid culture.

Under the leadership of Alfonso Caso and Gonzalo Aguirre Beltrán, a new focus on the indigenous populations led to the formation of the Department of Indian Affairs in 1936 and the establishment of the Instituto Nacional Indigenista (National Indigenist Institute, or INI) in 1948, at least partially as a way to intervene in village issues.

By 1952, INI headquarters were opened in the Department of San Cristóbal de Las Casas, with Alfonso Villa Rojas serving as the director. Representing a vast modernization and empowerment program for Indians, INI was organized within a legal and constitutional framework that gave Indians no special juridical status and was based on the explicit assumption that modernization would gradually lead to their absorption into the dominant culture. As with the American Indian Movement (AIM) in the United States, it was also part of a larger resurgence of ethnic nationalism throughout the world. The concept of "pluralism" emerged in Mexico during the 1970s with the declaration that, among other things, Indian peoples have the right to maintain their own myths of origin, which would then have to be factored into public interpretation (Gutiérrez 1999:110).

Official attitudes on indigenismo can be found in Mexican history textbooks and in museums, as well as in the national passion for archaeology. The masses of Mexicans who visit their country's great archaeological sites attest to the influential foresight of Benito Juárez, as do other cultural symbols, including the numerous historical murals and the performances of Ballet Folclórico de Mexico (van den Berghe 1995:570).

Mexico's definition of who qualifies as indigenous rather than as mestizo has been based on cultural and linguistic criteria. At present, census definitions utilize the cultural characteristics of individuals and not their communities, using criteria such as whether an indigenous language is spoken or, somewhat more quaintly, whether an individual wears shoes or sandals or goes barefoot. Even though as many as 80–85 percent of Mexicans are part Amerindian, they are classified as nonindigenous in the census unless they admit to speaking an indigenous language. Currently, the Mexican government formally recognizes more than 50 indigenous groups as indígenas (the Spanish colonialist designation of *indio* now carries a negative connotation).

According to van den Berghe, indigenas make up the most politically, economically, and culturally marginalized sector of Mexico's population in at least three ways: almost all peasants are landless and without political power; many of them are unfamiliar with the Spanish language and lack access to formal educational systems; and they are marginalized in the ecological sense because their populations are mostly concentrated in remote regions (1995:570–571).

Land redistribution and communalization, as seen with the Mexican ejido system, followed a class model until the political climate changed again in the 1980s, when it was recognized that indigenous peoples could vote at both the state and federal levels. This quickly proved to be an incentive for aspiring politicians to curry favor among them (van den Berghe 1995:570–571).

An appropriation of Indian-ness called "planned acculturation" was required for recognizing their very existence, and this change helps to explain why the formality of respect for Indian culture was included in the process of Mexicanization. Some have even argued that Mexico's postrevolutionary indigenist policies actually created the institutions that eventually became dedicated to satisfying the demands of tourism (Gutiérrez 1999:107–108). Furthermore, the early emphasis on the recording of archaeological and anthropological data in lieu of acculturating the different Indian cultures helped to push the movements of indigenism, nationalism, and anthropology into something of a crisis owing to the inherent incompatibility of playing on Indian-ness as a means to achieve a mestizo nation (Gutiérrez 1999:107–108; Palerm 1975:164).

The designation of mestizo has come to imply a rising above the sociocultural situation of the Indians, who remain at the bottom of the socioeconomic ladder, but it has also stimulated some ethnic groups to form their own intelligentsia. The cultural history of the Mexican Indian has become closely intertwined with the emergence of the mestizo culture, and both are clearly products of a colonial history that began with the conquest (Gutiérrez 1999:23–44).

3 Heritage and Archaeological Tourism in Mexico and Quintana Roo

As with the four S's (sun, sea, sand, and sex) of mass resort tourism, Valene Smith (1996:287–300) has coined the four H's of cultural or heritage tourism. Habitat refers to the geographic setting and underlying platform for the visit, whereas the term *history* implies postcontact relations between Westerners and aboriginal groups. Handicrafts manufactured by indigenous groups commemorate a visit and signify the market demands of tourism. Heritage is used to describe the body of knowledge and skills associated with individual values and beliefs.

The National Trust for Historic Preservation (2001) initiated the Heritage Tourism Demonstration Project in 1989, with the goal of securing a market niche for heritage tourism based on five designated principles and four key steps. The five principles are to find the fit between tourism and the community; to collaborate; to preserve and protect the resources; to focus on authenticity and quality; and to make the sites come alive. The four steps were outlined to begin a long-range strategy: to assess the potential; to plan and organize; to prepare, protect, and manage; and to market for success. These suggestions are helpful as a broad template for responsible heritage tourism, but, as can be seen in the Maya Riviera, they are easily sidestepped in favor of personal gain (Slick 2002:221–225).

Archaeological tourism, a variation of heritage tourism, is a particularly important economic asset for both developed and developing countries. In a study of public visits to three important archaeological parks in Mexico, Ernesto Beltrán and Mariano Rojas (1996:463–478) pointed out that visitors are not appropriately enjoying Mexico's enormous archaeological heritage. If services were improved, the perceptions of visitors would also improve. They advocate establishing self-financing mechanisms at each site, reasoning that if the public learns to value the preservation of archaeological zones, they are also more likely to contribute to the preservation of a particular site. As in the United States, budget problems within the Mexican government have led to reduced federal support for archaeological programs and necessitated a search for other funding sources.

Although international tourism has long been touted as a valuable educational experience, at least one study has raised serious doubts about the reliability of this conclusion. Results indicate that tourists tend to be poor culture bearers mainly because they have temporarily left behind their usual cultural roles as well as the symbols that would make them more understandable to others. In addition, tourists are usually concentrating more on hedonism and conspicuous consumption than on education and cultural understanding. "Tourism is very much about our culture, not about their culture or about our desire to learn about it" (Thurot and Thurot 1983:187).

Ethnocentrism, whether deliberate or not, often lies behind much of tourism's objectification (Hollinshead 1996:313) and can be recognized in the discourse on cultural or heritage tourism industry as much as in the tourist encounters themselves. A "culture-bound" individual who does not have the ability to empathize with the situations encountered in other societies may demonstrate ethnocentrism in the obvious sense, or it may be expressed in their different worldviews. It is also considered ethnocentric when indigenous peoples are represented by false or vulgarized images and when the heritage of indigenous populations is either rewritten or excluded altogether (Hollinshead 1996:314–315).

Tourism Development in Mexico and Quintana Roo

Mexico has been blessed with a multitude of attractions for tourists, many of which are linked to the four well-known lures of sun, sand, sea, and sex (Pi-Sunyer, Thomas, and Daltabuit 2001:122). The marketing of the four S's has proven to be more important for tourism growth than Mexico's rich cultural heritage, as shown by the Mexican government's reliance upon tourism to accomplish economic growth and regional development and for solving certain social problems such as illiteracy and unemployment.

Three distinct patterns of Latin American tourism development have characterized intensive coastal-resort development. One form of tourism development utilizes "primate" cities that have earned an international reputation within the tourism market and serve as entry points for many types of tourism. Examples of this type include Mexico City and Buenos Aires, Argentina. Another type is represented by destination resorts such as Rio de Janeiro in Brazil, which caters mainly to an urban, domestic tourism market. A third form, often called the urban-nodal plan, is representative of development around the Cancún area and is characterized by intensive coastal-resort development that has been extremely successful in attracting an international tourism market (Weaver 1997:81). Indeed, this plan has been so successful that development has recently been extended to the south and north along the coastline, as well as into the interior of Quintana Roo. La Costa Maya (the Maya Coast) now reaches from Tulum to the Belize border.

The primary form of Mexican tourism has changed over time to concentrate on the sun-and-sea segment, and by 1989, Cancún was the single largest tourist destination in all of Mexico (Call 2001; Clancy 1999:12–13). Only about 10 percent of Mexican tourism is primarily cultural or heritage, so the remaining 90 percent sun-sand-sea variety concentrates on a dozen or so major resorts collectively called "Club Mex" (van den Berghe 1995:568–599).

The Mexican government is extremely tourism conscious, having made enormous initial investments to augment extensive foreign capital investment. By concentrating mainly on the mass tourism market, several Mexican states have installed their own tourism offices with a number of schools dedicated to training personnel for the hospitality industry.

Until the introduction of mass tourism in the early 1970s, Quintana Roo (which became a state in 1974) remained much as it had been for centuries, which was an extensive region with a very low population density made up of mostly Maya forest dwellers in the interior and small mixed enclaves along the Caribbean coast.

The offshore islands of Cozumel and Isla Mujeres were the first tourism destinations to be developed in Quintana Roo. This small-scale tourism development allowed more profits to remain with the island residents and encouraged a more accommodating relationship between tourists and their hosts (Daltabuit and Leatherman 1998:320). When this proved successful, a group of government departments, including the tourism ministry (SECTUR) and the national development trust fund agency, Fondo Nacional de Turismo (now known as FONATUR), spearheaded the planning and construction of five new resorts in Ixtapa, Los Cabos, Loreto, Huatulco, and—the most successful of them all—Cancún (Call 2001; SECTUR 1991, 1992). With the common goal of international mass tourism, various state agencies did the planning, buying, and selling of land for development, provisioning the infrastructure, and local governance over the development. Clancy (1999:10–17) makes the case that the development of these resorts would not have been so successful if the state agencies had not taken such a proactive role in overcoming the many different problems as they arose.

Despite spending tens of millions of dollars on infrastructure, Quintana Roo was not initially successful in finding enough private sector investors (*New York Times* 2001). The state then came up with a two-track strategy whereby it was necessary to build and operate their own hotels at the same time that they encouraged price incentives for the private sector by offering preferential loans. To this end, FONATUR both guaranteed and subsidized loans for hotel construction (Clancy 1999:10–12; FONATUR 1993). At the same time that oil reserves were discovered in the early 1970s, allowing Mexico to become one of largest net oil exporters in the world, the early success with tourism development helped to make continued import substitution viable.

By 1974, development in Cancún had effectively attracted numerous foreign investors, and plans now called for three stages of construction over the next ten years or so. This momentum helped regional development to flourish until 1982, when a national debt crisis changed the economy drastically. Since then, state development strategies have alternated between austerity and structural adjustments before officials ultimately committed to a long-term emphasis on fully integrating with the world economy (Clancy 1999:12). Quintana Roo's industry was market-based, mainly controlled by the private sector, and oriented toward exports, with centers such as Cancún attracting about three-quarters of its visitors from abroad. By 1989, Cancún had become the single largest tourism destination in the country (Clancy 1999:12; SECTUR 1992).

Foreign investors were able to stay afloat during these changes because foreign hotel chains fit under equity ceilings set by a 1973 foreign investment law, ensuring that by 1978, Mexico was the developing country with the highest number of foreign-affiliated hotel rooms. As Clancy says, tourism had not only become big business in Mexico but, more important, had become a Mexican big business that was frequently allied with international capital. One estimate was that by 1987, 71 percent of the top two classes of hotels in Mexico were tied to foreign chains. This prompted aggressive and prolonged state action to produce the successful tourism business found in Mexico today.

Prior to the early 1970s, Cancún, a small village with a little more than 40 inhabitants, was used primarily as a base for hunters and *chicleros*. It was selected for large-scale government-sponsored tourism development because several very specific qualities were found there: beautiful beaches, the average annual temperature of the air and sea, the potential for building large hotels, the travel distance from various points of origin, and the number of cloudy days per annum (Brown 1999:298; Daltabuit and Leatherman 1998:320).

Cancún's resort development began in the early 1970s, spearheaded by the government tourism development entity FONATUR, in collaboration with the state of Quintana Roo. As related by Fred Bosselman, Craig Peterson, and Claire McCarthy in their book *Managing Tourism Growth* (1999), representatives of a number of integral departments agreed to a set of ecological regulations for the development of the Cancún-Tulum corridor (the stretch of road leading south from Cancún to the archaeological site of Tulum along the Caribbean coastline).

Launched in 1994 as the "Ecological Ordering Plan," it was designed to reduce the negative impact of tourism development along the Cancún-Tulum corridor. Ostensibly involving national, state, and municipal cooperation, the plan was based on a mapping technique that divided the corridor into 46 separate land zones and 28 different marine zones. Each zone was assigned a level of usage that was labeled either "Actual" (varying urban development and industrial use), "Conservation" (small rural or tourism development designed to protect wildlife), or "Protected" (use must be compatible with existing ecosystems) (Bosselman et al. 1999:127–128). Each designation specified whether a particular section of land was suitable for development or needed protection, or some combination of the two, as agreed upon by the agencies. For instance, the area inland to the west of the

Tulum archaeological zone was designated as a "conservation" area, limiting local development to no more than 15 rooms per hectare (Bosselman et al. 1999:128).

The development plan was linked to a financial structure organized in 1969, giving authority to FONATUR for the administration of a development trust fund. FONATUR was supposed to use funds from the Mexican government; however, the total initial development investment was $70 million, of which $30 million came from the Inter-American Development Bank and $20 million came mostly from foreign private investors (Pi-Sunyer, Thomas, and Daltabuit 2001:129).

New investment plans included several thousand additional hotel rooms over the next few years, reflecting the trend in the late 1990s toward environmentally oriented tourism in luxury accommodations and gated communities. Recently, there were no less than three controversial proposals to build large ports at Xcaret, Playa del Carmen, and Puerto Morelos, respectively, which would allow a minimum of 800,000 new tourists to visit the peninsula each year. Construction began for the Puerta Cancún–Xcaret Home Port as a joint venture between Carnival Cruise Lines and the Mexican owners of Xcaret Ecoarcheaological park to allow large cruise ships to dock at the park, where officials will be able to process as many as 10,000 people an hour (Travel Weekly 2001; Williams 2003).

In January 2003, plans were officially approved to provide docking for around 30 luxury liners each week. Promoters of the home port have argued that cruise ships already dock nearby on a gravel port so building a home port will make Mexico a major player and not just a provider for cruise ships, the fastest growing segment of the tourism industry (Williams 2003:A4). Promoters made the case that the project would benefit Maya Riviera communities because Carnival Cruise Lines promised to donate a share of the disembarkation fees to the local government to provide for regional education and health care needs.

In opposition, environmentalists decried the potential damage to the Great Maya Reef (the second largest in the world) by these massive ships and warned that the new influx of tourists would push the indigenous Maya even farther into poverty (Call 2001; Los Angeles Times 2003a). To prepare for home port construction, Xcaret's owners transplanted delicate coral using highly advanced technologies, which violated current environmental laws (personal communication, January 2003).

The Xcaret Home Port proposal created an unlikely opposition alliance among Maya Riviera residents, environmentalists, Maya rights activists, and established tourism business providers. Collectively, they have charged that the home port plans threatened the Maya Riviera economy as much as the environment. There was a real concern that the cruise ships would lead to a reduction in flights in and out of Cancún's airport and further reduce the occupancy level of the region's 46,000 hotel rooms. Further, since cruise ships don't employ local citizens or pay local taxes, any drop in hotel occupancy rates would result in a loss of jobs. Since the Maya Riviera generates 80 percent of the local economy and 40 percent of Mexico's total tourism revenue, these losses would be devastating and widespread (Williams 2003:A4).

A market analyst for the Cancún tourism industry, who also heads a hotel chain, represents another unlikely partner in opposing the home port. He claimed that too many hotel rooms already go unfilled, so bringing in 30,000 more tourists by ship each week will only make matters worse for hotels and business owners. Others were worried that the building boom and home port plans were ruining the getaway-from-it-all market that made tourism there so successful in the first place.

The Puerta Cancún–Xcaret Home Port aroused calls for Mexico's environmental agency to conduct a review before construction commenced, and several press releases called for action, stating that home port plans violated environmental protection laws, beginning with the failure to publish an announcement of development plans in a major newspaper. Other violations threatened the protected coral reef, as well as the endangered sea turtle colonies. Further, it was charged that the Manifest of Environmental Impacts also violated the law by failing to inform the community of the planned development. Carnival Cruise Lines was fined more than $30 million for nonrelated pollution violations, but Mexico's lack of strict environmental regulations assured that pollution from cruise ships would continue. Perhaps most alarmingly, construction continued even though the developers had never paid for the initial permits. It went to the Federal Fiscal Tribune of Judicial Power to consider the matter, and there the plans ended.

The other two home port proposals are independent from the one at Xcaret. Playa del Carmen's proposal was for a home port that would better serve boats going to and from Cozumel. Plans were made to transform the quiet town of Puerto Morelos into a major yachting destination by building a home port capable of berthing another 300 boats. At present, the fates of these other two home ports remain unclear, but at least one environmental group, Comité Local para la Imagen y Promocion de Puerto Morelos (Local Committee for the Promotion of the Image of Puerto Morelos), works to oppose, or at least mitigate, the construction of any enormous home port in the region. As with the Xcaret Home Port, land was cleared, some mangrove swamps were leveled, and a historical railroad once used for the production and export of *chicle* (the resin from the *chicozapote* tree used to manufacture chewing gum) was threatened with destruction, even though the necessary official permits were never issued.

A preliminary FONATUR report details future plans for three new "cities" along the Cancún-Tulum corridor, expanding the north-south highway, and constructing two rail lines. While some environmental groups have specifically objected to the destruction of the vegetation to build the rail lines, they, "admitted planned growth was preferable to uncontrolled, helter-skelter development as has been going on until now" (Garcia 2000).

The gap between rich and poor continues to grow in Quintana Roo, which already has a higher than average infant and maternal mortality rate, a lower than average age-at-death rate, and one of the highest rates of divorce in Mexico. Anthropologist Ana Juárez (2002:113–114) writes that the state of Quintana Roo has experienced the highest growth rate in all of Mexico, yet despite its reputation as one of Mexico's wealthiest states, it is also home to some of the nation's poorest and most malnourished residents.

Some would suggest that the tastes of tourists may already be veering away from the mass tourism-oriented luxury hotels in Cancún's Zona Turista and Maya Riviera enclaves, as opposed to a steady growth in the cultural tourism and ecotourism markets (Passariello 1983:109).

For the Mexican government and its major investors, Cancún's mass tourism development has been a resounding economic success, and plans for further development proceed despite widespread awareness of the many problems associated with mass tourism. That said, the Cancún model is still being replicated elsewhere, as evidenced by "The Cancúning of Cabo," the title of an article in the travel section of the *Los Angeles Times* (Beyette 2003:L1–3), which describes growing concerns that overdevelopment and high prices will drive away tourists to the popular Mexican Pacific coast resort town of Cabo San Lucas in the Gulf of California. In a discussion about what has been learned from the successes and failures at other prominent tourist destinations, Cabo San Lucas residents have expressed growing alarm about the depletion of game fish and not long ago won a battle to restrict commercial fishing to 50 miles offshore (Call 2001). One activist group, Defenders of the Bay, also successfully opposed a large dock for cruise ships that now must continue to anchor offshore (Beyette 2003).

Cancún's population now has more than 400,000 residents, with an annual growth rate of more than 20 percent (Daltabuit and Leatherman 1998:320). The period of the greatest growth was between 1976 and 1978, but growth has held at a steady rate since 1986. Perhaps Cancún could more accurately be described as two cities: the Zona Turista and the Ciudad Cancún, which is the city proper. According to FONATUR (1993), Ciudad Cancún was originally designed to serve as a secondary tourist center and for housing tourism industry workers, who would enjoy all of the essentials for modern living, including schools and health facilities. Strict environmental zoning regulations were to be enforced, except that these zoning plans never actually went into effect. At one point early in the development, Mexican government officials announced that they had brought in a team of anthropologists to help lay out the city in an effort to avoid potential social tensions, although there is little evidence of this plan today (Pi-Sunyer, Thomas, and Daltabuit 2001:129). FONATUR continues to function as the agency responsible for promoting tourism development but appears to have all but abandoned the early plans for public services and environmental safeguards (Call 2001).

Of the more than 2 million tourists arriving in Cancún each year, a number of them will travel down the coast and into the interior countryside. The coast from Cancún to Tulum is now home to an almost continuous array of resort hotels, timeshares, and vacation homes with restricted access to the beaches. Virtually every available beach has been claimed by large resorts, often with nondescript housing for their service personnel situated in the background nearby (Daltabuit and Leatherman 1998:320; *Los Angeles Times* 2003a).

In many ways, Quintana Roo has become an economic extension of the United States or Europe, with a whopping 91 percent of the tourists who visit Cancún arriving from the United States. Most of them are young (averaging thirty-six years of age) and relatively wealthy (with annual incomes ranging from $65,000 to $75,000) (FONATUR 1993:12; Pi-Sunyer, Thomas, and Daltabuit 2001:129). Major investors, often expatriates from the United States or Canada, control many of the beachfront enclaves where at least some resorts consume huge quantities of the available fresh water and put a strain on the region by operating with inadequate sewage facilities. Community protests against these inequities have had little effect so far, although an argument has gained some momentum that those who are the key extractors of resources should be held accountable as development continues (Gomez-Pompa and Kaus 1998:6).

Quintana Roo's Caribbean coastline has turned into "a veritable tourist factory" with numerous luxury hotels and theme parks, say Pi-Sunyer and Thomas (1997:187). The most prominent theme park, Xcaret Ecoarchaeological Park, remains a highly controversial and self-styled natural history theme park, where Within the park, ancient Maya archaeological buildings are treated as opportunities for amusement and unfettered exploration in the model of Disneyland attractions. The idealized Maya world at Xcaret is repugnant to many archaeologists, although it is touted as a source of revenue for the region and is very popular with the public, including middle-class Mexican families (Schuster 1999:88).

La Ruta Maya

Without question the most ambitious multinational ecotourism plan, La Ruta Maya (the Maya Route), became the focus of tourism development in the early 1990s. La Ruta Maya is a concept first proposed by William Garrett, former editor of *National Geographic* magazine, as a new approach to forging multinational cooperation. The proposed route includes territory that is home to several million Maya, thousands of archaeological sites, pristine forests, jungles, and wetlands (http://www.peoplesguide.com, November 2002).

The International Ruta Maya program involved a joint agreement among Mexico, Guatemala, Belize, El Salvador, and Honduras to promote ecotourism and salvage the few remaining patches of Mesoamerican tropical rain forests. The presidents from the five countries met together in 1989 and agreed to share jurisdiction over the Maya territory in order to inaugurate the massive tourism plan that included a 1,500-mile-long road linking the five countries (Daltabuit and Pi-Sunyer 1990:12). La Ruta Maya was featured in the October 1989 issue of *National Geographic* magazine, although many have derided the coverage as an attempt to promote the notion of tourism as a benign force with the noble goal of preserving the ancient and modern Maya (Daltabuit and Pi-Sunyer 1990).

Conceived as a top-down economic plan in an area that contains many Maya ruins and nearly 8 million native Maya speakers, the main project was devoted to the concept of ethnic tourism and the intention of halting the pillage of archaeological sites and saving the remaining patches of rain forest. In the spirit of cooperation, all five participating governments agreed that the region would benefit more from the renewable resources of ecotourism and ethnic tourism than from logging and ranching (van den Berghe 1995:570–571).

La Ruta Maya eventually evolved into El Mundo Maya (the Maya World), encompassing a 1,500-mile-long circuit connecting many different Maya sites. Regrettably, the project has never been completed and most of the goals have never been met, even the two main priorities of consolidating the already popular tourism centers and creating new integrated tourism resorts (Schluter 1994:254).

Of special note, a "Behind the Scenes" section of *National Geographic* (August 2003:n.p.) reported that earlier that year, the Inter-American Development Bank was able to induce the five nations of Mexico, Belize, Honduras, Guatemala, and El Salvador to join with the National Geographic Society, Conservation International, and Counterpart International in creating the Mundo Maya Sustainable Tourism Alliance. The express goal was to assist in building and maintaining tourist attractions in a way that would enable the Maya and other indigenous peoples to earn a decent living and help to preserve the environment.

Anthropological Theory as It Applies to Archaeological Tourism

In the influential book *Hosts and Guests* (1978:2), Valene Smith described a tourist as a "temporarily leisured person who voluntarily visits a place away from home for the purpose of experiencing a change." Nelson Graburn accepted this description of tourism, adding that structured breaks are characteristic of all cultures, and the ritual of tourism can be attributed to most, if not all, societies. In Graburn's view, tourism allows a separation from normal life in order to experience, however briefly, an alternate life that meets different mental and cultural needs (1983:11). Erve Chambers (2000:20–32) added that tourism provides cultural endorsement for renewal and re-creation, in which the end product is the experience itself. Ultimately, tourism is a mediated activity where the tourism industry not only accommodates tourists' desires but also creates new opportunities and new expectations (Chambers 2000:123).

Using questions originally posed by Michel Foucault, So-Min Cheong and Marc L. Miller (2000:372–373) supported the premise that power is a pervasive factor in the phenomenon of tourism. Current political analyses offer two broad categories, the first devoted to public policy and planning, and the second concerned with political economy and development studies. Both categories reflect how power is exercised and negotiated within the dynamics of tourism.

Another view on the mixing of anthropology and tourism comes from Quetzil Castaneda's incisive examination of tourism development around the archaeological park at Chichén Itzá. In his book *In the Museum of Maya Culture,* Castaneda made the point: "But anthropology and tourism have not simply imposed 'culture' onto Maya peoples as the frame through which they and we experience their sociality; rather, it should be added that the Maya have invented the anthropology (and tourism) of Yucatán. Maya participate in this invention as active agents or subjects in the guise of informants, workers, and 'real culture-bearers,' as objects engaging and contesting Western knowledge, as the pretext of investigation, and as ideal representations of alterity that are refashioned in Western imagination" (Castaneda 1996:9).

For Erve Chambers (1997:2), the most fertile ground for anthropological discourse lies in that precarious space between condemning the consequences of modern tourism and understanding the pervasiveness of the tourism industry. As such a prevalent and powerful force, it is fertile ground for anthropologists to examine the complex cultural implications associated with it. Since culture continually changes, it must be analyzed in relation to those ongoing changes, not only for how tourism affects culture but, equally, by how culture affects tourism.

Similarly, MacCannell (1976) said that tourism is a product of modernity and leads to homogenization, instability, and a loss of authenticity, until there is a quest for the opposite of these things. After all, anthropologists may just be the ultimate tourists, although some might argue that anthropologists more accurately reflect a rather extreme category of tourism.

Batya Weinbaum (1997:19–29) described important socioeconomic changes in a paper titled "Disney-Mediated Images Emerging in Cross-Cultural Expression on Isla Mujeres, Mexico." Although there are many different stories for how this small island off the coast of Cancún got the name of "Island of Women," the prevalent female imagery now includes likenesses from Disney animated films, especially Ariel, the little mermaid. These influences on Isla Mujeres may be seen as "transitional" rather than "traditional" because islanders have consciously chosen these images for commercial and capitalistic purposes rather than the more "authentic" local Maya imagery. The representations of women on Isla Mujeres are not the short and strongly built Maya women painted on ancient ceramic vessels; rather, commercial representations of Maya women now feature tall and thin sexual objects with abundant cleavage, which Weinbaum (1997:26) interprets as an example of how cultural imperialism from abroad has distorted local ideas about feminine beauty.

General Tourism Theory

"Travel is fatal to prejudice, bigotry, and narrow-mindedness, and many of our people need it sorely on these accounts. Broad, wholesome, charitable views of men and things cannot be acquired by vegetating in one little corner of the earth all one's lifetime." (Twain 1869:521)

An International Year of Tourism was declared by the United Nations in the late 1990s, when there was optimism that travelers from wealthier countries would positively contribute to the economic advancement of developing countries. In response, a number of developing countries jumped on the tourism bandwagon without doing adequate research into other alternatives and potential consequences (Britton 1979). Since then, it has become increasingly clear that tourism is not such a secure growth industry because it is highly susceptible to economic cycles, world events, and fickle tourist trends.

Various social classes experience tourism differently, which is an important point because there is plenty of evidence to support the contention that gaps between the rich and poor are getting worse. Tourists from wealthy nations also bring wasteful behaviors into extremely poor communities, sometimes fostering class resentment among indigenous peoples (Bodley 2001; Brohman 1993; Cothran and Cothran 1998; de Kadt 1978). Tourists travel to developing countries because they are less expensive, and they are less expensive at least in part because of local poverty. These and other problems are easily mirrored in the Maya Riviera where the gap is widening between wealthy property owners, foreign tourists, and indigenous populations.

Travel is generally thought to be enriching by contributing to a more open-minded and sophisticated attitude about one's place in the world. Until the advent of jet travel, only the privileged few had both the time and the income to be able to travel for leisure. Now, travel is so popular and affordable that it is seen as something of a cultural necessity for personal renewal.

The origins of tourism go back at least as far as ancient Greece and Rome, where wealthy vacationers soaked in thermal baths and traveled throughout Europe. Harkin (1995:655) has connected the word *tourism* to the French word *tour*, meaning to circle around, which has significance for understanding the nature of tourism. Now, tourism is an integral part in the economies of more than 100 nations and is probably the world's largest industry, having created more than 200 million jobs globally. With an estimated $3.4 trillion gross annual output from the more than 500 million tourists traveling in 1995 (Cheong and Miller 2000:372), international tourism has grown by more than 57 percent in the past decade and is expected to continue at an equally astounding rate in the near future. This is especially true in developing countries, where ecotourism opportunities offer both cultural and natural attractions (Hawkins 1994:262).

Tourism is usually described in economic terms as an industry and, as such, has been examined and documented in the same ways as other world industries such as agriculture. In an article titled "What Are Travel and Tourism: Are They Really an Industry?" Thomas Lea Davidson (1994:22) argued that it is viewing tourism as an industry that has contributed to so many misunderstandings in tourism discussions. In economics, an industry is often defined as "a group of independent firms all turning out the same product"; therefore, when considered as an industry, "tourism" refers to business interests that incorporate the specific economic interests of hotels, restaurants, transportation infrastructures and amusement venues. Tourism might just as easily be regarded as a social phenomenon because it produces an experience that is essentially expenditure-driven rather than receipts-driven (Davidson 1994:21–25).

Tourism Theory as It Applies to the Maya Riviera

It is reasonable to assume that a steady influx of cash from tourism will raise the standard of living and produce local jobs. Upon closer inspection, however, a large portion of tourism dollars do not remain in the region but are instead "leaked" back to wealthy, often foreign, investors. Some benefit goes to local and national economies through wage employment, entrepreneurial activities such as hotels and concessions, park entrance fees and local taxes, but most of the profits do not stay in the region.

The multiplier effect, as described by economists, occurs when the revenue generated from wage employment, park entrance fees, and so on is then spent locally, creating a secondary market for food, housing, and construction (Chambers 2000:33–35; Honey 1999:88). In the Maya Riviera, the effect is relatively small because tourism development has resulted in an imbalance of power in which the poor receive low wages and few benefits as compared to the rich (Pi-Sunyer and Thomas 1997:105).

The Maya Riviera is now a tourist mecca where the contemporary Maya residents have become an ethnic minority. A few loosely organized Maya groups have begun to call for cultural recognition and a voice in local environmental and economic policies when related to regional development. Some Mexicans argue that their country has entered into a new phase of neocolonialism called *entrequismo* (handing over), because of the domination by foreign capital interests (Cothran and Cothran 1998:493). Charges of colonialism are also triggered by the confusion over Maya identities formed prior to the modern era as opposed to the identities currently presented to tourists (Crick 1989:330–335; D. Nash 1989; Sutherland 1996).

Mexico's Maya Riviera is now a major global destination, ranking tenth in world international arrivals and twelfth in tourism earnings in 1994 (WTO 2000). It is now one of the leading sources of foreign exchange for Mexico, and after agriculture it is the largest source of employment. Tourism is also Mexico's second largest generator of foreign currency, earning $4 billion in 1991 compared with oil, which earned $8 billion in the same year (Cothran and Cothran 1998:478). Because tourism is so much more profit-oriented than education-oriented, regional archaeological sites are always at risk of being used by special interest groups who rarely concern themselves with scientific methods and historical accuracy (de Tapia 2002:28).

In some ways, the Maya Riviera seems as much Caribbean as Mexican, especially because of the tropical climate, idyllic white beaches, turquoise water, and music and food traditions. What may be the Maya Riviera's most singular asset, differentiating it from other Caribbean tourism destinations, is the allure of the Maya archaeological sites. Cancún and the Maya Riviera are also distinguished from other popular tourism destinations by other factors, not the least of which is that so many workers from other regions in Mexico and Central America have come to work in the tourism trade. In addition, the continual flow of international tourists has somewhat homogenized the region where the number of tourists and expatriates outnumber the native residents on a daily basis.

Cenotes and Caves in the Maya Riviera

Cenotes and caves have fascinated amateur explorers and treasure hunters ever since the spectacular collection of gold and other priceless artifacts was dredged up by Edward Thompson's exploration of the Sacred Cenote at Chichén Itzá almost a century ago (Andrews and Corletta 1995:101; Thompson 1992). The region quickly became legendary as popular books recounted the discovery of great treasures and told tales about sacrificed virgins and great warriors (Tozzer 1941).

Because cenotes were often the sole source of water for many ancient towns in eastern Quintana Roo, they occasionally shelter the remains of miniature temples and platforms as well as more commonplace water vessels. Local diving groups have from time to time recovered cultural remains, but they rarely report their finds. Near Tulum, Carwash Cave was explored by cave divers in 1986, where they identified a hearth at a depth of 27 meters (Andrews and Corletta 1995:105; DeLoach 1986; Lockwood 1989:136, 141). Subsequent analysis of recovered charcoal samples has provided a Late Pleistocene/Early Archaic date (uncorrected) and suggests a much lower sea level at that time (Andrews and Corletta 1995:105).

Quintana Roo's central coastline has numerous inlets and coves that probably served as harbors in pre-Hispanic times, several of which are also adjacent to archaeological sites (Andrews and Corletta 1995:106). Xel Há has one of the largest inlets, where a sizeable defensive wall, causeway, and shrine were identified about 10 kilometers from Tulum.

Shipwrecks have also been investigated along the eastern coastline, including the famous wreck of *El Matanzero,* a Spanish merchant ship that ran aground on a reef about 4.5 kilometers south of Akumal on February 22, 1741 (Andrews and Corletta 1995:106). Such shipwrecks often become embedded in living coral reefs, making both the ships and the reef vulnerable to damage by overly adventurous underwater exploration.

To date, the potential impact of underwater diving has not been extensively addressed in the literature, although the Society for Historical Archaeology held a conference on historical and underwater archaeology in 1987 to consider the serious threat posed by looting in the Caribbean. They eventually published a set of cultural resource management guidelines for the protection and management of maritime sites (Parrent 1988).

In 2002, El Primer Congreso de Arqueologia Subacuática y Espeleologica (Inaugural Conference on Underwater Cave Archaeology) was held in both Akumal and Mérida. Its purpose was "to discuss issues of proper conservation before an audience of both archaeologists and cave divers." This conference wisely chose to invite dive enthusiasts as well as underwater and cave archaeologists in order to create a dialogue about issues of mutual concern. In addition, the 2002 Cavern Guide training handbook, published by the Riviera Maya Association of Dive and Watersport Operators (APSA), also briefly discussed these issues (Rissolo, personal communication, June 2003).

At least a few popular guidebooks describe the excitement of underwater exploration of cenotes and shipwrecks in the Yucatán, but they only briefly allude to the problem of looting. For example, this narrative was found under the subheading for diving in the guidebook *Hidden Cancún and the Yucatán:* "Strangest of all is to dive a cenote, the region's remarkable deep natural wells. Many are swirled with murky waters, where blind fish wriggle through the darkness. But other cenotes have water as clear as liquid air, making them marvelous for diving. Dive shops can point you to the best cenotes. (Those at archaeological sites are off-limits to prevent looting)" (Harris 1999:64–65). Current publications, both academic and popular, suggest there is fairly high level of awareness among divers about the fragility of reefs, shipwrecks, and underwater archaeological sites, which it is hoped will continue to increase in the coming years.

4 Living in the Yucatán Today

In this chapter I look at the present-day Maya who face the pressures of tourism and modernization mainly because they live near archaeological sites in Quintana Roo. Special attention is paid to my own and other ethnographic research in local communities. The term *modernization* is used in a more general sense for this analysis rather than as a shorthand for economic and development theory. For this discussion, modernization incorporates the social, economic, and political processes by which societies adapt to new technology and new ways of thought. It also is part of the globalization process as Western influence permeates even the most remote parts of the world as well as part of an ongoing scholarly debate about the loss of traditional cultures.

Without doubt, the Maya in Quintana Roo are inundated by challenges to "modernize," and, in general, they say they want many of the material things that we in the United States take for granted. As soon as they can afford it, Maya families buy televisions and install plumbing and telephones in their homes. Even the *huipil,* or traditional dress, which is so well suited to the tropical climate, may become a thing of the past. Ethnographers report that after they begin to wear Western-style clothing, Maya women rarely revert to traditional styles, and Maya men tend to wear Western clothing earlier than women.

Many regard any change in a traditional culture as "culture loss," even though the one constant of culture is that it always changes. Who gets to decide which traits are to be changed and which changes are to be resisted? Unless change is forced upon the Maya, which few would legitimately support, the Maya have to make these decisions for themselves in response to the pressures of modernization.

One of the most pernicious aspects of modernization is that television, films, and magazines constantly promote the attitude that everyone wants the products being pushed by the media. Western standards of beauty, style, and attitude are continuously portrayed in both blatant and subconscious messages. Just as young people in the developed nations of North America, Asia, and Europe aspire to the imagery, so too do the Maya. By studying the pressures and effects of modernization on the Yucatec Maya, we have learned more about those same pressures on our own local communities and subcultures, although the Maya response may show a little more discernment. It is tempting to view the process of modernization as inevitable, but the Maya have proven to be resilient and resourceful for more than a thousand years and will likely find their own way to adapt to the world today.

The Yucatec Maya

The current circumstances facing the Yucatec Maya result from selected historical and political situations that help to explain their reactions to tourism development. Until the 1930s and 1940s, the state or federal government owned most of the land in Quintana Roo. During that time, the indigenous Maya were organized into *ejido* groups, who were granted communal ownership and control over particular land allocations (Galletti 1998; Cornelius and Myhre 1998; de Janvry, Gordillo, and Sadoulet 1997). At that time, the most important source of income in the region was chicle extraction; therefore, each *ejidatario* was awarded 420 hectares of land, or enough land to supply chicle extraction to support one family.

Each ejido was obligated to conserve and manage the forests under their communal control until the 1960s and 1970s, when even more land was allotted to the ejidos, albeit without the previously required obligation for conservation. Although the new land allotment effectively promoted the clearing of land for agriculture, the earlier allotments still acted to conserve large segments of land. A long-term conflict between the ejidatarios and the timber industry eventually led to policy changes in the region, resulting in local farmers becoming heavily drawn into the timber industry. For a time, the Maya earned income from both timber and chicle extraction, although there has been a steady decline in the production of both resources in recent years, without an alternative replacement. During that same time, the Maya have become minorities in their own homeland because so many other people have migrated into the state in search of jobs (Cornelius and Myhre 1998; d'Arc 1980; Hervik 1999; Oppenheimer 1996).

Not surprisingly, the Yucatec Maya exhibit little consensus about the processes of modernization, and Betty Faust (2001:155) has explained that attempts by outsiders to understand their range of emotional reactions become complicated by an age-old Maya propensity to hide their thoughts from outsiders. Some Maya villagers will even deny they speak a Mayan language, or they will identify themselves as agriculturists, or campesinos, rather than as Maya, possibly to divert interest. A number of anthropologists working in Quintana Roo have reported a response of "both adaptation and resistance" to modernization forces, in that some Maya choose to live primarily in traditional communities, while others attempt to move fully into the modernized world. Still others attempt to negotiate between the traditional and the modern (Juárez 2002; Pi-Sunyer, Thomas and Daltabuit 2001:126).

Anthropologist Ana Juárez (2002:18) reports that the Tulum pueblo Maya hold contradictory views about the process of modernization, especially as to how they see themselves in the "tourism era." The Tulum Maya articulate that while their traditional values are still important, they also need to earn cash to be able to live in the modern world. Further reflecting upon their contradictory perspectives, Juárez

(2002:120) noted that they usually prefer American dollars, which they sometimes ironically refer to as *dolores,* the Spanish word for "pains." During the "tourist era," the Tulum Maya say, their lives have become harder because of the need for cash, leading Juárez to conclude that they are criticizing their place within the globalizing system as much as the process of globalization itself.

Those at the lowest end of the socioeconomic ladder in the Maya Riviera are among those who see tourism as an opportunity to earn cash and acquire some of the trappings associated with modernization. While expressing genuine concern for the speed and pervasiveness of regional development, the Maya also see this expansion as offering the best opportunity for an improved standard of living, even if it means discarding some aspects of their Maya identity. More than a few Maya express the opinion that merging into the non-Maya world is not necessarily a bad thing and that replacing certain Maya values and attitudes with the values and attitudes shared by much of the rest of the Western world is probably a worthwhile trade (Hostettler 1996, 1997, 2001).

This attitude of accommodation contrasts starkly with the viewpoints of other local residents, both Maya and non-Maya, who express concerns about the considerable environmental problems connected to extensive tourism development. Interviews reveal pessimistic predictions about where the development of the Maya Riviera is heading. Anthropologists and biologists also express great concern for the overall fate of the region, a concern that is combined with a sad resignation that the force of modernity may simply be bigger than any group can resist. Some Maya have expressed ambivalence about the opportunities for education and careers that have steered them away from their Maya heritage, saying that they find themselves in a no-man's-land between the Westernized, developing world and their traditional Maya heritage.

Television has had one of the most profound influences on modernizing Maya villages since the early 1990s (Pi-Sunyer, Thomas, and Daltabuit 2001:136–137), when 67 percent of the households in the town of Cobá were found to own televisions, with many families watching up to six hours each day. In Mexico, television is closely associated with political power, especially by reinforcing the national stereotypes of hypermasculinity and individualism. Television especially highlights the outside world, which is also the world of the rich and powerful tourists, and tends to make the Maya feel even more marginalized and dissatisfied (Pi-Sunyer et al. 2001:136).

The Maya Capacity for Syncretism

The imposition of a foreign religion onto an indigenous population has historically been seen as a destructive force. Most groups try to resist such an imposition; however, the Maya have been particularly adept at finding ways to combine their ancient beliefs with an overlay of Catholicism in many creative and manageable ways. Syncretism, the term for a blending of ancient and Christian religions and rituals, has contributed to Maya adaptability over the centuries and is fundamental to understanding how they currently respond to the challenges of modernization.

The temple cult is probably the most visible, blended element of Maya religion, where ancestral gods and agricultural deities coexist with the tenets of the Catholic Church. For example, the Maya sun god has been identified with the Roman Catholic version of God, the corn god is associated with Jesus, and the moon goddess, *Ix Chel,* is transformed into the Virgin Mary (Pearce 1984:156). Three distinct patterns of religious practice guide modern Maya worship: attending to the old pantheon of deities who control the economic and ecological status of the community; adhering to the agricultural cycle; and preserving the forest and its natural resources (Pearce 1984:xii).

Most Maya families continue to claim Catholicism as their official religion, although the church is not always the greatest moral force in their lives. Some Maya say they are more often guided by the traditions of their ancestors. In particular, the Maya believe that the forest is alive with spirits who own and protect their individual domains. Ceremonies in honor of ancient deities are still performed regularly in the Yucatán, Chiapas, and Guatemala. *Ch'a chaak* is a particularly important ritual performed to awaken the *Chaaks* from their winter sleep so they will bring the annual rain to nourish newly planted seeds (Pearce 1984:xii–xiii; Press 1977:281; Redfield 1950:114–115; Villa Rojas 1988:125). On the other hand, Daltabuit and Leatherman (1998:324) have reported that the ch'a chaak rain ceremony, as with other traditional agricultural ceremonies, is in decline largely because the reliance on agricultural production is also in decline as men spend more time working in wage-labor jobs.

Ancestor worship is another important religious component, although this seems to be more highly developed in the Highlands than in the Lowlands of the Yucatán Peninsula (Pearce 1984:xiii). Principal symbols of the temple cult are the *santos,* renamed for Christian saints who often serve as effigies for some of the old Maya deities. In addition, the ancient cross remains a potent Maya religious symbol for the world's first tree and is still placed at village boundaries and on the occasional hilltop shrine (Pearce 1984:5; Redfield 1950:123; Villa Rojas 1988:127–130).

The symbol of the cross has been a central religious motif for the Maya going back to the earliest days of creation and certainly was in use before the arrival of Europeans. It could be seen as the last surviving symbol of a cosmic-centered faith that deified the earth, the sun, and all forms of life. In this way, the Cult of the Talking Cross in Quintana Roo may represent a religious cult where the Maya appealed to deities of a higher order than those of fields, forests, and other elements of nature (Burns 1996; Jones 1977:xxii; Leon-Portilla 1988; Pearce 1984:41).

Maya religious traditions are maintained by folk priests, who are believed to be appointed by the ancestors to perform the principal duties of curing illness and see-ing to the general welfare of the community (Pearce 1984:15–19). The Maya also believe in prophecy, particularly prophecy that helps them understand and explain present and future events. The most outstanding historical prophecy may be the one predicting the arrival of the Spaniards and the overthrow of the ancient gods. Occasionally, it is repeated that faith in this prophecy played a key role in the Maya acceptance of Spanish domination, although it was more likely fabricated as propa-ganda after the conquest.

Protestant missionary groups are becoming a greater influence on Yucatec com-munities, particularly Pentecostal, Evangelical, and Mormon Christians. Ethnog-raphy on the Maya community of Cobá revealed that until about 20 years ago, the Maya practiced a religious folk syncretism. But now, Cobá has five or six compet-ing religious congregations, most conducting evangelical services solely in Span-ish and placing emphasis on individual salvation and a personal relationship with God. Unfortunately, these changes also increase cultural differentiation within the community and further undermine the long-held communal ties and rituals (Pi-Sunyer, Thomas, and Daltabuit 2001:132–135).

Conversations with Yucatec Maya Women

Numerous interviews were conducted with residents in Quintana Roo, as a way to gain insight into various perspectives on tourism development and what different people think about the public's interest in the ancient and modern Maya. The fol-lowing conversations are with Maya women, all in their early thirties and living in the Maya Riviera region, yet who now find themselves in markedly different life circumstances. To protect their privacy, I have labeled them as Maya Woman #1, Maya Woman # 2, and Maya Woman #3.

Maya Woman #1

Although she lives in the Joaquin Zetina Gasca colonia, next to the town of Puerto Morelos, her particular work brings her into contact with a variety of issues and many types of people. As a botanist, she expresses great concern for the loss of coastal vegetation over the last twenty years as land has been lost to development.

Culturally, she observes that the Maya used to depend upon one another, but this has lessened with rapid development of the region, most of it related in some way to tourism promotion. As a professional botanist with a fulfilling career, she ex-presses feelings of insecurity as she faces the constant threat of further development on the grounds of the botanical garden. Perhaps the biggest threat to the garden comes from the fact that not many people visit, even though its location along the busy federal highway seems an ideal location. Politicians regularly propose plans to encourage more visitors by building restaurants and bars in the garden.

The politico-economic status of the botanical garden can be expressed as having "an enemy inside the house" because the state of Quintana Roo has the option to take the land at any time. She told me that she has tried for more than a decade to maintain a productive relationship with various government agencies, but it is a tiring position to be in and not without personal sacrifice. She says she continues her work for the benefit of her sons' generation, but the demands are such that she must be away from home too much of the time. Her work is often frustrating because even when she is able to convince government agencies with her data, they often approve a project only to ignore its actual implementation (personal communication, July 30, 2002).

The botanical garden is still under threat even though there has been both local and international support for the garden's value in the conservation of local plants. The value of the plant collection and understanding of local Maya botanical knowledge has gained respect and support throughout the world. Yet only about 3,000 visitors come to the garden each year, mostly students and some tourists, and without a budget to promote the garden, the significance of political liaisons was not recognized until recently. School field trips are offered free of charge, and the garden is beginning to offer the site as a venue for workshops for international groups, especially for botany aficionados and bird watchers, as a way to augment funding. An outreach program has been initiated in which botanists and other researchers will visit schools and town meetings to explain the important work going on at the garden.

Not many Maya visit the garden, as evidenced by the lack of signage in Yucatec Mayan, although there are numerous signs in Spanish and English. There is an interest in mounting an interpretive program that would provide a more direct link between the modern Maya and traditional Maya knowledge of the plants and animals found within the botanical garden. She has been working with a pueblo near Felipe Carrillo Puerto on the curative value of various indigenous plants with plans to offer workshops on using medicinal plants for curing illnesses, delivering babies, and promoting the continuation of a more traditional Maya lifestyle. The objective is to bring Maya people here to perpetuate Maya lifeways although there are many big obstacles, not the least of which is that few Maya live close enough to the garden to be able to visit regularly.

Heritage is seen as a valuable product to develop even here in this protected space. According to her, big investors don't understand the nature of Quintana Roo but see only the heat, humidity, snakes, and mosquitoes. It is as "silly" to transform Quintana Roo into a place where nature is restrained and passive as it is for tourists to adhere rigidly to the routine of beach, hotel, and bars. In the botanic garden, a visitor has the rare opportunity to learn about indigenous birds, plants, and seasonal diversity in the tropics, and it is surprising to her that there is so little interest.

From her point of view, she has the uncomfortable yet essential position of representing the Maya heritage to garden visitors. Since she has a university degree and is the only staff person fluent in both Spanish and Yucatec Mayan, she works with eight other Maya employees to present an evocative picture of Maya life. She expressed tremendous gratification at being able to work with these eight Maya men as they have taught her many things about living in close proximity to the forest. She says she has learned to move about the forest without fear by learning some survival skills and is quite appreciative of this opportunity to live in the forest "as if in a house" (personal communication, July 30, 2002).

She expressed a feeling common among the Maya of being disrespected when politicians and investors bring up the Maya name in marketing discussions. She wonders where the Maya populations have gone during all of this development. Once there were many Maya communities, but they now live in small pocket communities on the outskirts of towns stretching all the way from Puerto Morelos to Chetumal, as exemplified by the *colonia* that lies on the inland side of the federal highway near the town of Puerto Morelos. There are also problems with the ejidos, as outside investors have been conceded large extensions of ejido land even though mostly Maya continue to live on these lands (personal communication, July 30, 2002).

The botanical garden is also home to a few Maya ruins, collectively called El Altar. When visitors come to the botanical garden, there is no signage to provide information and few people ask about them. Since the staff has little pertinent information available on the ruins, they are generally left as a backdrop for emphasizing the botanical and biological specimens. The staff claims to have too much work to do to maintain the garden in any case, so there is no time to take advantage of the archaeological component on the grounds. When asked whether visitors ever wonder about possible links between the ancient and modern Maya, she answered that few ask and those who do inquire seem to be satisfied with vague answers. Occasionally, a visitor will ask the botanical garden staff, "Where are the Maya now?" For a while, she arranged field trips to the nearby colonia to visit a traditional Maya group; now, however, that group has disbanded, and there is little to offer in answer to such a question.

She gladly related details of her own childhood in a very small town in which Maya traditions and language were practiced daily. There was no television or electricity, and as children they were free to play in the orchards and forests around the town. It was at this time that she became curious about the fruit trees while her brothers were out making *milpa*. It was a case of "little house, big land" with her childhood spent outdoors amid the trees. A very good student, she had the opportunity to attend college in Chetumal, even though this meant that she had to leave her beloved home town in order to live in the city. For her, it was a tough life in a poor neighborhood filled with unsavory people. In spite of this, she managed to graduate and develop professionally, eventually securing her job at the botanical garden. Being a student had cost much of her self-esteem as many of her neighbors seemed to regard her as swimming against the tide and opting to get away from her Maya life. However, her work at the botanical garden and the cycle of life as lived through plants was a curative for her, and she managed to adapt swiftly.

She says her Maya husband has not enjoyed the move to the colonia of Puerto Morelos, as he prefers to live in the city as far as possible from the persistent insects. By contrast, her life in the colonia and her work in the botanical garden remind her of her tranquil childhood, which she wants to replicate for her own sons. She attempts to maintain a simple lifestyle, without hypocrisy, which remains very important to her.

There is some pressure to represent the Maya as a liaison with the developing world, but she says she is only trying to repeat her childhood lifestyle, which was "right" for her, and she hopes that it will also be "right" for her own sons. Her life's work, both at home and in her career at the botanical garden, has evolved into "a talk that never ends" (personal communication, July 30, 2002).

Maya Woman #2

In the same Joaquin Zetina Gasca colonia, another Maya woman is grappling with different issues. This woman has lived in her cinderblock house for thirteen years and works three days a week as a housekeeper for an expatriate American woman with two adopted Maya children. For this three-day workweek, she reportedly earns about 450 pesos each week (about $42). She has three children, the oldest of whom is a twelve-year-old girl.

Her house has had electricity only for about a year, and they must continue to draw their water from a well, although there are plans to provide households with drinkable water within a couple of years. Being able to use electricity was a great improvement in many ways, not least because the gas used for lamps and the stove gave her terrible headaches (personal communication, July 2002).

In her thirteen years in this colonia in Puerto Morelos, she has seen many changes to the area. Not long ago, it was all jungle and laden with mosquitoes, but over the years people have been migrating into the community from areas as far away as Oaxaca and Veracruz to search for wage-earning jobs. She claims that these groups are compatible, and, because they live in the same community, face the same challenges, and hope for the similar lifestyle transformations, they become rather homogeneous.

Her family comes from the Maya community of Chemax in Quintana Roo and although other residents, from Chiapas for example, also identify themselves as Maya, she is unable to understand their languages so they speak Spanish to communicate with each other. She says her children understand but are unable to speak Yucatec Mayan. Because her mother-in-law lives with the family, there is some continuity in observing Maya traditions, but such traditions are no longer considered to be important in the larger community. There is an attitude of laissez-faire involving a renegotiated identity that is intricately connected to the ambitions of the diverse residents here.

As for school curricula, her children are now taught something about Maya history and culture, but courses are taught in Spanish and there are no provisions for teaching Mayan. She is now thirty-one years old and learned the Spanish language while in school, although she spoke Mayan with her parents at home. She was never taught about the ancient Maya civilization or about the long cultural continuity of the modern Maya people. When asked if she had ever visited any ancient Maya archaeological sites, she replied that although she had visited Chichén Itzá and Tulum, she was most familiar with Cobá because she had uncles who lived in a nearby town.

Her Mayan-speaking parents live in a *palapa* without electricity in the inland Maya community of Chemax, where they still cook on a wood-burning stove, tend to a home garden, and raise chickens. At her home in the Puerto Morelos colonia, her family is able to earn better wages than people in Chemax because the milpa no longer brings in enough to eat and farming is too erratic to depend on. Before moving to the colonia in Puerto Morelos, her husband had no land for milpa because he was sick and missed the deadline for filing papers with the ejidatario. Now, he is disabled and cannot work. She and her mother-in-law agree that factors around this disability have led to her husband conducting an affair with another woman in the colonia, causing upheaval and stress for her family (personal communication, July 2002).

It is regrettable that she cannot bring her children to visit their grandparents more often, but the cost of the bus trip is about 400 pesos (a little under $40) round-trip for each person and the total is prohibitive for the family. Her eighty-five-year-old mother-in-law is also able to earn some money by washing clothes for an American expatriate at a rate of about 25 pesos a day (or 35 pesos if the clothes are very dirty) (personal communication, July 2002).

She and her mother-in-law have converted to a Pentecostal religion and have put aside their Catholic and Maya traditions. They consider themselves to be devoutly religious, pray often, and now claim to bring the first fruits of their harvest to the Christian God, much as others present them to the aluxes in a milpa. When asked what their church thinks of those long-held Maya traditions, she tells about little stone houses that have been built along the boundaries of the milpa in which to place offerings for the aluxes, and according to traditional Maya recitation, were actually built by the aluxes themselves. She says the church supports this practice because so many feel the aluxes at least protect the milpa from mice, if they do nothing else. By contrast, her natal family in Chemax sustains a belief in aluxes and continues to offer the first milpa harvest to the aluxes to protect against retribution in the form of fevers and other illnesses. They don't see themselves so much as losing their traditional Maya lifestyle as gaining additions to their lifestyle to improve their lives. She expresses the hope that her own children "will grow up better than the way she grew up" (personal communication, July 2002).

Compared to the frequent tourist interaction experienced by Maya Woman #1, there are few opportunities in the colonia for contact with tourists. She thinks their interest in the region can only bring more opportunities for families such as her own and expresses the opinion that the buildings constructed for tourism are very pretty and she would like to see them expand even to her own colonia (personal communication, July 2002).

Maya Woman #3

Another perspective comes from the experience of a woman thirty years of age, who lives on ejido land in Central Vallarta in Quintana Roo. She came from the town of Valladolid fifteen years ago and now lives with her husband and two sons, eleven and fourteen years old, in a partially renovated Maya palapa. She is a very industrious woman who sells elaborately embroidered clothing to tourists who occasionally pass by her house while on a jungle tour. When asked her opinion of tourists, she sighs and then smiles as she replies that their presence benefits her because they pay cash for her clothing and are very nice people. She says that she would like to see more tourists visit her ejido as long as she has things to sell, primarily because this provides her with cash to meet her family's needs. She has seen the area change a lot in the last fifteen years, particularly in that more people are moving there and more trees are being cleared from the land.

As a schoolgirl in Valladolid, she was never taught about the ancient Maya, although she reports that her sons' school curricula has included lessons on Maya prehistory. Her sons must live in Puerto Morelos to attend high school, and her fourteen-year-old recently dropped out of school because he felt disconnected from his family. It is her hope that he will return to school by the next school year.

Even though she speaks both Spanish and Yucatec Mayan, her husband speaks only Spanish so her sons have not been encouraged to learn her native language. Since her parents speak only Mayan, this makes it difficult to establish a meaningful communication when she and her sons visit them in Vallodolid every two or three months. Even though she lives next door to her in-laws, she does not speak to them as she regards them as immoral and ruthless when dealing with other people.

When asked about perpetuating Maya traditions, she relates that her sons are not very interested when she initiates discussion as "they are far away from those things" (personal communication, July 2002). She does burn copal and make offerings for celebrating the Day of the Dead by setting up a shrine with food and small gifts. The offerings attract her sons' interest, much as Christmas food and gifts do for American children, which she puts to advantage by placing the shrine next to the television. She told a somewhat humorous story about her insistence upon observing the Day of the Dead rituals. As she began to set up the shrine with candles and offerings, her sons were full of questions. Why did she go to so much trouble if the dead are truly dead? How does she know the dead will come to her shrine, and why does she waste food that will go uneaten? She tried to explain that the food offerings were meant to honor the dead and that her sons should be observant to see if there are any signs that the dead are visiting the shrine. As her sons watched the burning candles, a bag under the table rustled and her startled sons asked if this was a sign the dead were visiting the shrine. When she affirmed that it was indeed proof of a visitation, they compared the strange feelings they were experiencing and became convinced of the necessity for a yearly ceremony to honor their dead family members (personal communication, July 2002).

While discussing the impacts of modernization brought on by tourism development, a more sober story slowly emerged. Most of the time, her husband is a hunter, but he also occasionally works to help clear land for the milpas of other farmers. When it is the slow season for milpa, her husband must leave the family to work elsewhere so she must produce even more embroidered clothing to earn money. Recently, her family life became more difficult because her husband began an affair with another woman living in the ejido and stopped providing food for their sons. When their subsistence reached a critical level, she was forced to go to the ejidatario to intervene and force him to provide for them. Now he is again living with his family and providing for them, although relations remain strained.

Both of these women view their biggest challenge as coming from how their husbands' infidelities had compromised their family structures, which they connect in some way to modernization and tourism development.

As these women demonstrate, the Yucatec Maya have been able to rely on a shared religion and communal organization to maintain their cultural continuity over many centuries. Previously the threat came from the severe burdens imposed by colonialism, revolution, and rebellion. Now, the threats most immediately come from the commercial dominance of tourism and from Pentecostal missionaries who encourage the Maya to replace their shared, syncretic beliefs that have helped them to endure through so many other trials.

Other social changes are apparent in contemporary Maya communities, such as the pressure to work for wages rather than continue traditional maize agriculture. Opportunities to work in the tourism and construction industries put the Maya in competition with other Mexicans who have migrated into the region and make it necessary to learn Spanish and English to be able to compete for jobs.

The modern Maya face life decisions that are barely comprehensible to those of us who have lived our entire lives in the developed world. Most of my informants report their most pressing and immediate goal is to make a better life for their families, and they see the tourism and construction industries as the most direct path toward a better life. They say they are willing to make the sacrifices necessary to improve their situations, even if that necessitates making adjustments to their family structure and religious practices.

Whether the latest Maya adaptive response will inevitably lead to entirely replacing the traditional Maya lifestyle is not yet clear. Most advocates argue that if they are given a voice in the decision-making process, another adaptive response will arise that preserves the core Maya identity. Terry Rugeley has repeated the Yucatec adage *Bis u yutsil bej, bik xi'ikech ich k'i'ixil,* or "Go down a good road, not through the briars" (2001:199), and if the Maya are able to choose the road they are to go down, their choice will likely reflect their characteristically philosophical yet practical approach toward the future.

Local Maya Activist

An informal style of activism can be seen by the efforts of a Maya hammock maker and distributor, who described to me how he became so troubled by the accumulated trash on the local beaches in Puerto Morelos that he initiated a weekly Sunday afternoon beach cleanup campaign. His efforts arose from the realization that littering is unacceptable for maintaining a clean and attractive neighborhood, as much as from the insight that a dirty beach will be unattractive for the tourists who buy his hammocks (personal communication, August 2002).

He has lived in Puerto Morelos for the last ten years, although he was born and raised in a Maya village near Mérida, in Yucatán state. When he was about five years old, his mother told him that if he didn't learn to make hammocks he would have to sleep on the floor, so he has earned his living by making hammocks ever since. He was traveling all over Mexico to sell his hammocks before he came to Puerto Morelos, where he decided to settle down because he says he could see a big change was coming to the area. Even though Puerto Morelos has changed very slowly over the last several years, everyone is talking about changes on the horizon. He says an individual must have a voice in any local development so he has organized the Sunday beach cleanup and joined the Comité Local para la Imagen y Promocion de Puerto Morelos (Local Committee for the Promotion of the Image of Puerto Morelos). He was also instrumental in building an artisans' cooperative for the town, with a museum and an extra room for selling food and holding cultural activities (personal communication, July 2002) (Figure 17).

He expresses two potential problems with tourism development in Puerto Morelos. The most critical involves access to fresh water as there is only one well for the entire town. He cites the example of Acapulco, where major hotels consumed most of the water after it was developed as a major tourism destination. He also expresses concern that someone will want to build skyscrapers like those in Cancún

Figure 17. Maya cooperative in Puerto Morelos

but concedes that the economy is better when tourists come though town. He remembers when tourists stopped coming for a while after September 11 and have not yet built back up to previous numbers.

Although he lives in Puerto Morelos with his brother, his wife and two sons live in his home village near Mérida. He is able to visit them about once a month although he brings them to Puerto Morelos to enjoy the beach during the summer. He and his brother have plans to move their families to Puerto Morelos as soon as they are able to afford a suitable house.

He describes a sense of connection with the ancient Maya and boasts that he possesses the "energy of a real Maya." He says that it is possible to feel like a Maya only when he is far from civilization and that the feeling recedes when he is living in town. His sons are learning to speak Yucatec Mayan, in addition to Spanish and English, and he is proud of their achievements. In general, he says the Maya are changing in that they are no longer "shy" and now want to learn about the world (personal communication, July 2003).

Attorney

By all accounts, perhaps the single most significant change in regional social and environmental accountability has resulted from the establishment of a nonprofit environmental law office in the Zona Turista in Cancún. I was able to interview an environmental attorney who is part of a nonprofit group called the Mexican Environmental Law Center (mainly funded by American nonprofit organizations), which monitors the work of the environmental ministry and tracks compliance with Mexican environmental laws. His job is approximately equally divided into two approaches: to hold conferences with the hotel associations for instruction on how to comply with environmental laws and to file lawsuits on behalf of the public against those in noncompliance with the laws (personal communication, April 2003).

According to this attorney, the purpose of a home port is to place it in or near a city to launch cruises, much like a main station. Economically, it might make more sense to locate a home port where there is little tourism as a way to obligate people to spend money there rather than in an already developed area. However, the proposed location at Xcaret would obligate people to visit the park even though the park is already a successful financial concern, and it may even represent a strategy to make up for other investments that have not been doing as well.

Mexico designed its environmental impact laws based upon European zoning programs and made compliance mandatory (personal communication, April 2003). For example, it is legally forbidden to remove organisms, whether alive or dead, from the sea, although lawsuits have alleged that this is exactly what has been done at Xcaret and at Playa del Carmen. The Xcaret group received local permission to use a highly developed technology to move a portion of the coral reef to make room for cruise ships, even though the plan and the permission went against federal environmental laws.

In the early years of developing Cancún and the Maya Riviera, there were too few regulations in place to adequately enforce compliance. However, now there are many more regulations ensuring that noncompliance will increasingly be brought into the public arena, as when the plan to move part of the coral reef at Xcaret was made public. The result was that a number of people lost their jobs, particularly those who worked directly on the zoning program (personal communication, April 2003). Today, almost every part of Quintana Roo has zoning regulations that require leaving a certain percentage of natural land available and undeveloped, although this varies according to the area. Compliance has been made easier with a sort of checklist that seeks to avoid corruption, but of course there are ways to avoid these laws. In the Maya Riviera, the most typical tactic has been to build more rooms than were authorized, as shown by an important lawsuit involving the Mayan Palace resort. In this case, a permit allowed the Mayan Palace to be built in a precisely designated location with a limited number of allotted rooms, but it was actually constructed with many more rooms and in a location a full kilometer away from where the permit authorized. In such cases, the resorts are usually fined, although the fine is usually only a fraction of the income that will be derived.

This attorney also agrees with critics such as Daltabuit and Pi-Sunyer (1990) who charged that Maya Riviera resorts are not following appropriate sewage treatment laws, specifically a law known as NON002. In fact, he claims that literally every large resort development in the Maya Riviera is in noncompliance with at least a few environmental regulations (personal communication, April 2003).

Employment regulations are more strictly enforced than environmental laws, but he also concurs with the contentions of others that the Maya who are hired to work at these resorts often are forced to live in substandard conditions. Even when a resort builds new housing for workers, the housing is not big enough to house all the workers, and many must live in small cabins without electricity, sewage treatment, or access to clean running water. Colonia Colosia, which houses service workers for the Playa del Carmen resorts, represents the worst-case scenario of contrast between the extremes of wealth and poverty in the region. The highest salaries generally go to foreigners, while most of the Maya and other indigenous peoples work as gardeners, waiters, and maids at salaries of $200 to $300 a month at most (personal communication, 2003).

Another test case lawsuit involving Playa del Carmen was brought by an emerging nonprofit consortium of small hotel owners, scuba diving businesses, and fishermen. This group has been working together to stop plans for another pier proposed by a corporation called Aguaworld, with the intention of increasing ferry service between Playa del Carmen and Cozumel. In this case, the assessor made a serious mistake when filing the Environmental Impact Assessment, and the case was scheduled for a hearing in the courts, as were the lawsuits involving the Mayan Palace and the home port at Xcaret.

Traditionally, Mexican courts are not friendly to environmental matters, especially when it is difficult to determine the legal interests, and they will usually intervene only when there are issues of personal damage. Mexico's federal courts have not yet become accustomed to lawsuits involving environmental impact. Both the lawsuits involving the Xcaret Home Port and the Mayan Palace resort were before the Federal Court for Administrative Justice (an executive branch), and, if no resolution is found there, they will then go to the judicial branch, known as the Empire Trial. The attorney has introduced a new environmental law that has been passed in all other areas but was still pending at the Senate level at the time of this interview.

Human Rights Activist

As the owner of a small hotel in the Ciudad Cancún, this local activist uses solar power and recycled water and offers Tai Chi classes every morning. Also an activist with an organization known as GEMA (Grupo Ecolojista del Mayab), this individual is one of roughly a dozen people who work very hard to find "transcendent" solutions for environmental and social problems in the region. Over the past 20 or so years, this small group has worked to change people's minds, and in the past five years there is enough interest to allow them to organize groups in Chetumal, Puerto Morelos, Cozumel, Felipe Carrillo Puerto, Holbox, and Playa del Carmen. Each group functions independently but operates within the same guidelines and emphasizes working with the local press to educate the public about serious environmental and social problems.

Some regard the development of the Maya Riviera as another form of conquest for the Maya people because it has meant that they must leave their traditional lives to work in the tourism industry and abandon their traditional costumes to wear uniforms at luxury hotels. In those hotels, they become aware of the luxurious amenities such as air-conditioning, even in rooms that go unoccupied, while they must return to their homes without electricity or running water. Daily, they witness large amounts of wasted food, when at times there is not enough food for their own families. Many Maya families must live with as many as ten people sleeping in one or two small rooms without toilets or showers, while virtually every hotel room in the tourist zone has its own private bathroom. Most Maya service industry workers are paid less than foreign workers and are contracted on a month-by-month basis. This means there is no work in the slow season, so they are often able to hold jobs for only a few months each year. Even so, the minimum wage in this area is a little less than $4 a day, so they must depend upon tips to receive a decent wage. It is worth noting that even though this minimum wage seems impossibly small to Americans, it represents one of the highest minimum wages paid anywhere in Mexico (personal communication, April 2003).

GEMA has worked with Maya women in an especially promising project that helps them improve their opportunities by creating better quality crafts to sell to tourists. They made arrangements to have good sewing machines donated and trained the women to improve the quality of their products, which is a form of *capacitación* (empowerment) (personal communication, 2003). This represents a more satisfying plan that trains people with useful skills so they can work for decent wages.

Although the Maya have never unified, primarily because they come from so many different regions, labor rights may eventually turn out to be the most important social issue in the Maya Riviera. For instance, when a hurricane hampers the tourism market, the hotel owner may not necessarily lose money, but the worker loses hours of work and tips. Conversely, when it is high season and the hotels are full, workers do not get more money for their work. For local activists, it is not only a problem of changing laws but of changing minds, because even the labor rights laws that are in place lack sufficient enforcement. When hotels and businesses are fined for violating labor laws, they simply pay the penalties without changing their practices. Virtually every informant recognizes that there is so much money-laundering activity in Cancún that it is very easy to pay to solve your problem. "With money, the dog dances," goes the old Mexican adage (personal communication, April 2003).

Some nonprofit activist groups are limited in what they can say and do about environmental and social problems in the region, primarily because they have wealthy developers among their board of directors. GEMA has always felt it was better to be free than to be wealthy, so they have consistently refused donations from rich people as well as from government entities. Several years ago, GEMA received a large donation from the World Wildlife Fund, the first such donation made by the WWF to a group without a specific project. The donation was for GEMA to use for local projects over a five-year period, and there is pride that this grassroots organization remains independent of big business. This approach is highly most effective because they have been able to maintain their independence and are not beholden to any of the power brokers. It has also meant increased respect for GEMA, and even when they are at odds with other groups, they are eventually asked for help in resolving yet another problem (personal communication, April 2003).

Activists Against the Xcaret Home Port

The proposal submitted by the owners of Xcaret Ecoarchaeological Park and Carnival Cruise Lines for building a home port at Xcaret has generated a great deal of publicity and public outcry. As a response to this proposal and its seemingly inevitable implementation, an unlikely alliance of groups opposed to the home port was formed. One shared concern is for the Great Maya Reef just offshore from Xcaret, which had already been altered in preparation for allowing the cruise ships to dock onshore and disgorge thousands of passengers at a time directly onto the grounds of Xcaret Park.

In January 2003, two articles in the *Los Angeles Times* detailed the alliance of developers and environmental activists in opposition to the home port construction. I contacted the newspaper's journalist who wrote the story, Carole J. Williams, and a *Los Angeles Times* fact checker in Mexico City for information about setting up interviews with the constituents in opposition to the home port. Eventually, I was able to arrange an interview with a prominent member of the Asociación de Hoteles de Quintana Roo (Hotel Association of Quintana Roo), who at first glance appeared to be an unlikely opponent of home port plans to bring thousands of tourists into the region on a daily basis. Also at the interview was another official closely associated with the local administration of Cancún.

In a two-hour meeting in April 2003, these men expressed the point of view that there are many serious and negative ramifications for the area if cruise ships were allowed this degree of access. Their primary concern was that since cruise lines offer all-inclusive vacation packages, they do not add value to the area by renting locally owned hotel rooms or eating in local restaurants. They contend that cruise ship passengers will spend only an average of $55 each at a port-of-call, while a tourist who arrives by air will spend over $1,000. This means that although cruise lines do utilize the infrastructure and tourist venues in the region, they do not contribute to the economic growth. Additionally, 20 years ago, tourists who arrived by cruise ships were a different clientele than those who arrived by planes, but now they come from the same pool; therefore, they are directly competing with local businesses by advertising in the same newspapers and magazines. Cruise lines currently have the advantage because they are able to offer a package that averages about $200 less than a land-only package (personal communication, April 2003).

These businessmen feel that those who have worked to develop Cancún and the Maya Riviera over the last 30 years have also worked to build the infrastructure, but now the cruise lines want to cash in without contributing anything back to the region. Cruise ships do not pay sales or property taxes to Mexico or to the state of Quintana Roo, nor do they employ Mexican nationals, because in general, crew members come from Scandinavia and the Philippines. Onboard shops are duty-free and beer is sold at lower prices, as other examples of the disadvantages faced by local businessmen. Maya Riviera tourism income comes to about $3.6 billion each year. These businessmen estimate that the construction of this home port would have caused a loss of about 20 percent of their business, or more than $700 million annually, which would be detrimental to the entire region (personal communication, April 2003).

There are numerous reports about unfair labor practices that allow cruise ships to hire workers at extremely low wages and even more problems with the enforcement of environmental regulations for cruise ships at sea. According to these officials (personal communication, April 2003), because there are inadequate maritime environmental laws in Quintana Roo, cruise ships are able to drop their garbage at night when there is no one to stop them. This is a problem with maritime law everywhere in the world, but it is even worse in developing countries such as Mexico.

Carnival Cruise Lines might best be described as a monster-sized public company, offering more rooms than Cancún, Puerto Rico, and the Dominican Republic combined. After heavy lobbying with the state and federal governments, Carnival and the Xcaret group were given permission to build the home port, but there was strong opposition to the legislation at every government level, and a consortium of travel agents and chambers of commerce were prepared to take the case to Mexico's Supreme Court.

A centerpiece in the opposition's complaint was that the home port developers had not followed legal procedures, particularly in publicly informing local communities about their plans and eliciting a public response before the plans were approved. People were concerned that the Xcaret group had already transplanted live coral to make room for the cruise ships, which is illegal and should have been made public before rather than after the fact (personal communication, April 2003). Home port opponents argued that the permit was issued without regard to the legal requirement for public disclosure, and the plan further endangered a public resource that is federally protected. Another important contention was that the approved home port plans did not use the same geographic coordinates as the area slated for development, thus rendering the plans illegal.

Ultimately, developers share concerns that they will lose their competitive edge to cruise lines, especially in this difficult period of war and terrorism. They note that Americans are not flocking to Europe or the Middle East right now, but they are attracted by the shorter flights to the Maya Riviera that offer "affordable holiday packages, terrific weather, beautiful beaches, the second largest barrier reef in the world, and the most sophisticated civilization in the New World." In some ways, this region might even be a safer travel destination than the United States because there is never an orange zone declared in the Maya Riviera (personal communication, April 2003).

As of this writing, local activists and officials have scored a huge victory by heading off the Xcaret Home Port for the foreseeable future. In 2003, this standoff had assumed an almost David-versus-Goliath proportion, so this victory must provide a real boost for the local groups who banded together to stop it.

5 A Discussion of Problems and Potential Remedies

Over the 30-odd years of tourism development in the Maya Riviera, the pattern has remained the same: investors siphon off large sums of money, leaving only a little to trickle down to the lower socioeconomic levels where most Maya reside. Poverty is a real problem that needs to be addressed for the overall welfare of the region. Since the trickle-down method is clearly not working, it is necessary to find alternative strategies that work for all residents.

Many see tourism as offering the best solution for rescuing the poorest sectors of society, but the only jobs available for the untrained and poorly educated are still found in tourism and construction (which often offer only seasonal employment) or in the *maquiladoras* (small apparel assembly factories), which generally pay low wages and offer little chance for advancement. It is not difficult to find extremely poor neighborhoods in the region, although there may be, arguably, some evidence for a slowly emerging middle class in some areas of Cancún and Playa del Carmen.

Cancún may well hold the distinction of being the first city ever built exclusively for tourism purposes. This strategy is finally bringing the region to a crossroads because the growing resident population in Quintana Roo finds itself in competition for the same resources with an even larger population stream of visitors. The resident population is itself an escalating problem. For example, in 1950 the population density of Quintana Roo was only 0.5 persons per square kilometer, but by 1995 this had increased 34-fold to 17 persons per square kilometer (Juárez 2002:115–116). The expanding population presents a challenge to Cancún and surrounding environs to evolve into an urban area that is capable of meeting the long-term needs of all of its citizens.

The second problem is far less serious but nevertheless also merits careful consideration. This problem is attributable to the low-quality brand of mass tourism marketed in Cancún. To survive in a competitive and often fickle market, Cancún needs to promote a healthy range of tourism opportunities to avoid becoming judged as stale and unhip. Originally planned to appeal to families and groups from North America and Europe, Cancún was among the Mexican destinations marketed as an "infinitely malleable" dream destination for everyone (Alarcón 1997:179). It has been portrayed as an idyllic place where "a combination of sand, sun and fun, and the Riviera Maya, with its talcum-powder beaches, underground rivers, archaeological sites, and turquoise sea, suits most visions" (Cancún Tips 2001a:31). In recent years, continual pressure to fill hotel beds and restaurants has meant an increasingly low-end marketing campaign that caters to uninspired middle-class family holidays and drunken college students, earning Cancún a less appealing reputation.

The third problem, which is even less serious but still needs to be addressed, lies in the condescending attitudes many scholars exhibit toward tourism research. As a pervasive global phenomenon, tourism merits earnest consideration, if only to understand better what is and is not effective from the local to global level. Few would argue that most of Quintana Roo's troubles stem from badly managed tourism more than from tourism per se. What is difficult is changing both the perception and the operating system to tourism that is sustainable and beneficial to more than just the developers and investors. The tourism industry profoundly manipulates the region's social, environmental, economic, political, religious, and public health concerns and clearly merits intense scholarly study (DeVita 2000).

Tourists themselves also demonstrate a snobbish attitude toward tourism. Quite often, people are inclined to deny that they are tourists, or they may try to explain why they are not stereotypical tourists, further indicating the widespread bias (Waldren 1997).

Cancún continues to enjoy considerable success even though its development plans go back to a concept that was popular in the late 1960s and early 1970s, and tourist perceptions and expectations appear to be moving in a different direction these days (Friedland 1999). Scholars such as Pi-Sunyer, Thomas, and Daltabuit (2001:130) and others (Hillery et al. 2001) are correct in suggesting that the greatest changes in tourism are probably ideological and conceptual, especially since few modern tourists want to think that their visit will damage the region's ecosystem or will negatively impact the local communities. Tourists want to believe that their activities are benign or even beneficial to the locals.

My research employed two approaches for understanding the interactions between tourism development and local communities (Stronza 2001:263). The first approach was concerned with identifying the factors that explain local tourism development. The more obvious material attractions have already been discussed, as have the plans to bolster the economy of this former backwater state. It is not insignificant that Quintana Roo did not actually become a state until development was well under way, which allowed for a lot of leeway in avoiding various laws and regulations.

The enormous scale of marketing Maya Riviera tourism has thus far overwhelmed all other considerations. In certain respects, the region seems to be just now, metaphorically, catching its breath. It is crucial that officials soon begin to consider the social and environmental costs, and to ask whether the tourism volume and current rate of construction can properly be sustained at this pace. Moreover, if the social and environmental problems continue unabated, will tourists even continue to visit in such great numbers?

A second question was just as important to my research: how do the various kinds of tourism influence the attitudes and behaviors of tourists? My research suggests that the marketing strategy has thus far been successful for mass tourism because the tourism promoters have been able to offer an array of activities in a reasonably priced luxurious and safe environment. Mass marketing has played on the somewhat exotic atmosphere (yet with an American feel) for tourists who prefer to vacation in an atmosphere that seems somewhat familiar.

At present, the system has been slow to encourage a more serious alternative such as cultural tourism or to offer many ecotourism alternatives. The current practice is to bring busloads of tourists to archaeological sites, which actually encourages the perception that these sites are theme park attractions rather than heritage sites worthy of more contemplative exploration. In addition, by failing to adopt more innovative methods for presenting interpretive information at archaeological sites, tourists are encouraged to view them as another source of entertainment.

"A trip to Chichén Itzá may be experienced simultaneously as pleasure, education, work, adventure, and time travel" (Alarcón 1997:182). This blending of education and entertainment has even spawned a new word, infotainment, and is a growing trend in popular culture in many parts of the world. I am enthusiastic about getting the message out that archaeology can be both relevant *and* fun, but this must be accomplished in ways that express their value to humankind. Mexican tourism officials have made it a high priority to accommodate crowds at archaeological sites such as Tulum and Chichén Itzá but have missed the mark in making them both fun and relevant to visitors.

Limiting access to archaeological sites by issuing permits or by charging much higher entrance fees is not a practical alternative for officials. Even the most casual visitor can become inspired to learn more about the ancient Maya after visiting one of their ancient cities. In any case, these archaeological sites are still seen to embody Mexico's cultural heritage, and Mexicans continue overwhelming support for the idea that they remain accessible to the public.

A reliance on mass marketing, combined with a uniformity in tourism offerings, could be said to represent a curious failure of capitalism, likely because the entrepreneurs are not generally trained in either anthropology or tourism studies and don't understand what serious travelers need and want. Notably, certain other nations are building markets in heritage and ecotourism, so it would behoove Mexican officials to improve and expand the overall visitor experience in the Maya Riviera and tap into this trend.

Definitions of Tourism

Malcolm Crick (1989:331) asserts that tourism offers an alternate version of the "at home/not at home" perspective because tourism results in an inequitable socio-economic relationship between the host communities, which work to meet the needs of the vacationers, who have come to play. Grassroots enterprises have generally been unsuccessful, possibly because of a lack of access to business training classes and widespread marketing and because many of the best and brightest residents have left for greener pastures in Mexico City or the United States.

Perhaps the most serious marketing miscalculation by Cancún's tourism developers has been a lack of imagination about what else might be possible. Current marketing strategies offer few alternative forms of cultural tourism and ecotourism, but when tourists are interested enough to venture out on their own, they are usually able to find those alternative experiences and demonstrate the potential market for other tourism experiences. The Travel section of the *Los Angeles Times* (Pawlik 2003) described the tiny seaside town of Xcalak as an as-yet-undeveloped spot. The author urges a visit in the near future because the town is slated for development as part of the ambitious building plan, La Costa Maya (the Maya Coast), which is the stretch of coastline south of Tulum to the Belize border.

One example for more imaginative tourist offerings was highlighted in an article in *USA Today* (Clark 2003:1D) that introduced Freedom Paradise, a new resort in the Maya Riviera's beach town of Tankah that billed itself as the world's first "size-friendly" resort. The all-inclusive, all-you-can-eat resort aims to appeal mainly to American tourists, which is a sizable market because two-thirds of American adults are now considered overweight. Their slogan says, "Live Large–Live Free," and to accommodate their clientele the resort offers wider than usual chairs, showers, and walkways and even hires "size-friendly" employees.

Although tourism marketers occasionally look for new tourism niches to gain a competitive edge, Cancún continues to primarily attract a middle-class clientele who take advantage of group discount packages. Tourists interested in a more intensive cultural experience are more inclined to visit other regions, such as the Mexican state of Chiapas, home to the archaeological sites of Palenque, Bonampak, and Yaxchilán, where advertising has concentrated more on the region's cultural heritage. In the Maya Riviera, tourism developers acknowledge the need to broaden their customer base by offering experiences that are more individual and out of the ordinary, such as spa vacations, but this strategy aims to expand their established consumer base rather than replace it.

Some scholars, such as Smith (1989) and Chambers (1997), have concentrated their research on the benefits associated with tourism by stressing that it is a form of economic development that will eventually improve the well-being of everyone in the region. Smith (1996) has also argued that the benefits of tourism generally outweigh the potentially harmful effects.

Yet Alarcón (1997:183) claims that all too often, modernization is correlated with Westernization and brings along new social problems, such as increased crime and drug use. Many aspects of tourism are undoubtedly destructive, often in direct proportion to a destination's popularity, but the phenomenon is just too complex and too pervasive to be condemned or praised out-of-hand. Tourism has the potential to bring in at least a few concrete benefits to host communities, most obviously by introducing better access to health care, education, infrastructure improvements, and employment opportunities.

When Villa Rojas (1945, 1962, 1977) was working in the Yucatán, he reported that violence was endemic and that almost half of the babies born in Maya communities died in infancy. It is hard for those of us who live a privileged, modern lifestyle to imagine what it must be like to lose half of your children in infancy. Although this is no longer an everyday reality in Quintana Roo, high infant mortality remains a grim reality among poor, isolated Maya communities in Belize and Guatemala. In modern Quintana Roo, cases of malaria, dengue fever, yellow fever, and tuberculosis have almost disappeared, and children no longer die in great numbers.

The Maya I interviewed claim they now have more opportunities with tourism development, where before they were limited to subsistence farming, fishing, and occasional day labor. None of my informants expressed a desire to return to the days without electricity or indoor plumbing, and most maintained their hopes for participating in the modern world. They want to have a say, however, in how and when they are to participate in the modernization process.

In an article discussing modernization in traditional cultures, John Bodley (2001: 206) suggests that it is more relevant to ask whether economic development actually increases or decreases a culture's ability to satisfy the physical and psychological needs of its population. The standard-of-living measure of a community's well-being lacks a universal cultural relevance and has not always been useful. Instead, Bodley recommends looking at factors such as a society's nutrition and general physical health, the incidence of crime, family stability, and the relationship to the natural resource base, among other factors.

There is ambivalence among scholars about whether economic development has increased the Maya's ability to satisfy their physical and psychological needs. According to Rugeley (2001:198), the sentimentality of the early revolutionary indigenist movement at first promoted a respect for Maya culture and helped to lift the stigma of colonialism. As education and financial opportunities opened up, some Maya have begun participating in politics, and, perhaps more important, there is an emerging Maya intelligentsia of influential writers and artists. Notably, this intelligentsia has called for maintaining their cultural heritage while loosely linking all Maya groups together as a Pan-Maya movement, but they have yet to gain a strong political voice (Adelson 2000).

Some Maya ethnographers have carefully detailed many of the adverse changes in the Maya lifestyle, especially in their diet, general health, and family relationships (Brown 1999; Juárez 2002a, b; and Pi-Sunyer, Thomas, and Daltabuit 2001). When driving along the peninsula's back roads well off the tourist track, it is evident that there is still a great deal of poverty among the Maya all over the peninsula, not just in the Maya Riviera. Job opportunities in the tourism industry are usually low level and don't pay well, but it is instructive to contrast the situations of the Maya who work in the Maya Riviera with Maya who live in areas as yet untouched by tourism. Overpopulation has also become a stumbling block in rural Yucatán, where agriculture is no longer a viable option for such a large labor force and there is increasing competition for land.

My informants acknowledge that the comforts that come with modernization are matched by nostalgia for the way things used to be. Moreover, my research has found that the Maya continue to place great value on the qualities of generosity and reciprocity in their communities, which they do not yet see as having been significantly compromised by modernization (Juárez 2002).

Culture Change

Understanding culture change is integral to understanding tourism development, particularly among indigenous communities. As noted by Valene Smith (2001:17), the process of acculturation often keeps pace with tourism growth, and as the speed of tourism development accelerates, so do the technological adaptations. As previously suggested, the brand of mass tourism that was popular in the 1970s reflected a commercial shift from jobs in manufacturing to the service industries (Alarcón 1997; Juárez 2002; Mowforth and Munt 1998; Pi-Sunyer, Thomas, and Daltabuit 2001). The wealthier citizens of Quintana Roo have already adopted the status symbols attached to consumer consumption in the same ways that consumerism is an integral part of the lives of Americans, Europeans, and Japanese.

Mexico exemplifies a nation that is industrializing and mainstreaming into a consumer-based system with a labor force that is slowly beginning to accumulate the discretionary income and time to travel. Another perspective is that Mexico's economy is a race between development and population, with tourism as the primary development strategy and the cultural, archaeological, and natural resources as the local attractions (Pi-Sunyer, Thomas, and Daltabuit 2001:127–129).

Will the Maya become integrated into this trend? If so, how long will it take? Momentarily setting aside the widely shared misgivings about the incredible speed and scale of Maya Riviera tourism development, another question looms: what will happen if the tourism industry goes into a sudden decline due to anxieties about economic woes or safety concerns? What happens if the region simply becomes less popular with tourists? What alternatives will be readily available for all those who have come to depend upon tourism for their livelihood? Will it mean a large movement of people out of the area, as has happened in the distant past? There are few satisfactory answers to these questions other than the reasonable assumption that many people will leave, and those who remain will likely revert to the subsistence agriculture of the pre-tourism era (Adelson 2000; Montague 1997).

Unfortunately, switching back to agriculture may no longer be practical, given the realities of population growth and competition for land and other resources. As early as 1948, ethnographer Robert Redfield (1950; Redfield and Rojas 1962) reported that villagers in Chan Kom were complaining about the need to shorten the swidden cycles because of increasing populations. Go "forward with technology," was Redfield's recommendation (Redfield and Rojas 1962:178), but the subtext was that population size was already becoming an issue 60 years ago, and the trend away from subsistence agriculture has greatly accelerated since then.

In the book *Where Asia Smiles,* Sally Ness (2003:232) analyzes the local response to tourism in certain towns in the Philippines, concluding that an adaptation to tourism development is "not producing an absolute rupture with the identities or practices, or the people and institutions, of the plantation culture that precede it." Furthermore, she notes evidence that agricultural practices are already changing whether or not communities are involved with tourism, much as the changes are already taking place in Quintana Roo.

Culture change that is generated from within and controlled by the group itself implies something very different from change that is imposed by outsiders. After all, choice is only valid if it is freely made. The Maya have a long history of adjusting elements of their culture to meet the needs of a changing environment, and my hunch is that they will eventually adjust to the tourism era.

Commercialization of the Maya Image

For most Mexicans, and indeed much of the rest of the world, the term *Maya* has become an added value for consumers. It has been appropriated as an exotic brand name that can be experienced only in this part of the world. Xcaret Ecoarchaeological Park provides a good example of a venue that many say capitalizes on a contrived and inauthentic representation of the modern Maya. That they have been so successful suggests that most visitors don't share the same concerns about authenticity as do archaeologists and other scholars. Or, is it because it's the only game in town that offers a Maya cultural experience to everyday tourists?

Before Xcaret was transformed into a theme park, the area was described as one of the most magical places on earth, "with water so clear and still it could not be seen as water until a stone was dropped into it." As construction began, dynamite was used extensively to create artificial lagoons, underground rivers, and a large sandy beach area. Coconut palms and other plants were brought in such large numbers that the landscape was completely altered. Modifications were even made to some of the archaeological buildings, including planting bougainvillea to make the site appear more picturesque.

Local activists recount a revealing conversation with a powerful local developer who spoke about all his accomplishments in life and how much wealth he has accumulated. Aspiring to leave a legacy, he declared that he wanted to build a large volcano, big enough to be seen from the land and from the sea. The land around the volcano was to be filled with little "mayitas," so everyone would be able to see the daily lives of the modern Maya. "Like monkeys?" he was asked, to which he replied, "Yes, I will put in monkeys too." Although the volcano was never completed, the remnants can still be seen from some distance away, and one cannot help but wonder what might have been accomplished if that money and effort had instead been invested in improving the lives of neighboring Maya communities. That would have been a true legacy that persisted over many generations, and might have, perhaps, set a precedent for other wealthy investors to follow.

Some environmental and social activists see it as their greatest challenge to find acceptable alternatives for integrating Maya workers into the modernized world. Television and advertising have convinced the Maya that they, too, need to have the accessories carried by tourists, and who can fault them for wanting to adopt a more modern lifestyle when the alternative often means living without access to electricity, running water, medicine, and an education?

Language is an especially critical hurdle for the Maya who are continually pressed to learn Spanish and English in order to qualify for jobs in the tourism industry. Yet, they are also frequently urged to retain their Maya identity. Access to education is probably the most basic and pressing need for the most disadvantaged Maya, but some activists would argue that the state and federal approach to education has not demonstrated much progress for indigenous peoples. A 1998–1999 fourth-grade science textbook details how indigenous peoples are the ones responsible for destroying the Mexican ecosystem through the use of the milpa system, which instills disapproval among Mexican children and causes shame among the Maya (personal communication, April 2003).

For me, the debate on authenticity is primarily academic, and most tourists seem more concerned with enjoying themselves than with whether something is authentic. Tourists to Cancún and the Maya Riviera expect to have a relatively inexpensive and fun-filled vacation in a beautiful area, as promised in their travel brochures. By contrast, Mérida is promoted as the place "where archaeology begins" on billboards along the main Maya Riviera highway. Still other billboards publicize Mérida as the place "where culture begins," thus playing off the flashy, superficial image of Cancún by stressing that Mérida is the place to visit if your goal is to have a unique and culturally rich experience.

Occasionally, an experience or performance will begin as a form of entertainment for tourists, such as Sunday folk dancing in the park in Mérida, until the performances evolve over time into a tradition that even the host communities may come to see as authentic (Anderson, personal communication 2003).

Along the Maya Riviera, the propensity has been to market everything, including archaeological and heritage sites, as commercial ventures above everything else. Directional signs along Federal Highway 307 from Cancún to Tulum help to blur the distinctions between the tourism venues, despite efforts to reduce the excessive and distracting signage. Official directional signs are a standardized deep green color with a white border, although several especially prominent signs have combined the venues of Xcaret, Xel Há, and the Tulum archaeological park on the same sign, connected by the sizable Xcaret logo. They are presented as if these destinations were all part of the same commercial package and even that they have a shared ownership. Not only do these directional signs include the logos of the commercial enterprises, but they list the commercial enterprises *before* they list the archaeological parks, which remain an integral part of the Mexican national heritage. Another consideration, as some have argued, is that the Mexican Secretariat of Tourism has been compelled to compete with theme parks and mega-resorts in response to the great success of Disney World and Epcot Center in the United States (Alarcón 1997:173).

By most accounts, the original development plans for Cancún and the Maya Riviera had solid, responsible goals and standards that took into account the sustainability of the region's ecological and cultural resources (Alarcón 1997; Mowforth and Munt 1998; Ochoa 1991; Pi-Sunyer et al. 1999, 2001). Nevertheless, the development plans that aimed to abide by appropriate laws and regulations, and the subsequent enforcement of those regulations, were never fully realized in Quintana Roo.

Lapses in enforcing laws and regulations can happen anywhere, but in the United States they are more likely to be investigated by the news media. Along the Maya Riviera, the same consortium that owns several local papers also owns the controversial amusement parks of Xcaret, Xel Há, and El Garrafón on Isla Mujeres. When scanning these local papers, it quickly becomes apparent that they are thinly disguised promotional advertising for local restaurants, hotels, and tourist excursions. Of note: there are several other local newspapers that do serious news reporting, most notably *Novedades de Quintana Roo, Por Esto de Quintana Roo,* and *La Voz del Caribe,* but they are more difficult to find in the tourist zone.

Until recently, there was little incentive for compliance and enforcement of the social and environmental laws and regulations that were put in place during the initial planning and initiation phases of development. However, in the last several years, the Mexican Environmental Law Center has become an established presence in Cancún that is funded by politically independent nonprofit groups. Since then, crucial lawsuits have been filed against a number of local developers who were charged with breaking environmental laws or violating building permits. Without a doubt, as affirmed by a number of environmental activists and hotel officials, the work of the Environmental Law Center has devised the single most effective strategy for holding developers accountable for violating laws and environmental regulations (Garcia 2003). It is an effective beginning that opens the way for other proactive voices to be heard.

6 Mexican Cultural Identity and Patrimony in Quintana Roo

The topics of cultural patrimony and cultural identity have been central to federal policies since the early years following Mexican independence. In the beginning, Mexico tried to play down the differences among the many ethnic groups in order to present a unified Mexican identity where everyone spoke Spanish and identified themselves first and foremost as Mexican. It was not long before the Mexican government replaced the one-identity plan with a policy that glorified Mexico's cultural diversity, and its indigenous groups in particular, at least partially because those ethnic differences were recognized as profitable for tourism.

The government's approach to marketing the nation's cultural and natural diversity for tourism meant that opening the first archaeological sites of Monte Albán and Teotihuacán to the public became, at least in part, a way to generate revenue. As a nation grappling with severe poverty and pressing environmental and economic troubles, archaeological sites were seen as resources requiring little in the way of upkeep. Since then, the official version of Mexico's national heritage has driven cultural patrimony by policies that continue to be integral to the political agenda.

Mexico's official attitude toward national heritage has also been a strong influence on how the nation's numerous archaeological sites and museums have been interpreted for the public. Because the sites and museums are not situated in equally accessible locations, a disproportionate burden is placed on those located near major tourist destinations. On occasion, states such as Chiapas and Campeche have collaborated with the federal government to enhance the visitor appeal in their state's archaeological sites and museums, but they are the exceptions, and most states have shown less foresight in choosing to augment federal funding to cultivate new and innovative programs.

Cultural Patrimony

Patrimony has been defined in Webster's Collegiate Dictionary as "anything derived from one's father or ancestors," but attitudes about cultural patrimony also tend to reflect the current political climate. A robust spirit of national patrimony initially inspired the assertion that all Mexican archaeological sites were fundamental to the national heritage, therefore they belonged to all Mexicans regardless of their ethnic origins.

Patrimony was also a factor in the establishment of the Instituto Nacional de Antropologia e Historia (National Institute of Anthropology and History, better known as INAH) as the monolithic national agency charged with the administration of all past cultural resources.

The earlier nacionalismo movement toward a unified Mexican people meant that indigenous languages were to be set aside and replaced with the Spanish language. Self-identification was to be Mexican without distinctions among ethnicities, although the mestizo tradition nevertheless promoted an identity that reflected a blend of Spanish with native genes and traditions.

The inherent contradiction could be seen as early as the 1960s when Mexico began a major renovation of the public education system by introducing the first collection of compulsory texts, which also happened to polarize the academic debate between the historical-culturalists and modernists (Gutiérrez 1999:1–2). The compulsory texts incorporated a cultural and political push toward nationalism that was intended to gradually transform the various ethnic groups into a unified and modern nation. During his first speech to the country, President Ruiz Cortines (1952–1958) contended that the education program aimed to raise the level of culture by introducing vigor into the Mexican identity and by orienting education to better serve economic development (Gutiérrez 1999:60). There was a determined push to instill a sense of a shared historical past, encourage cultural integration, and teach *patrias* (native land) as the supreme norm in which all citizens would eventually adopt Mexican-ness as their national identity (Ceniceros 1962:14).

A universal sense of Mexican-ness also meant reconciling the ideologies of the Hispanic and indigenous traditions that were reinforced in public arenas such as museums and archaeological parks (Gutiérrez 1999:60–81). These education policies are still in place, with textbooks continuing to favor the Hispanic version of Mexico's legacy, while minimizing the indigenous heritage. As an example, one official textbook mentions the existence of cultural diversity as part of the "many Mexicos" of the past but concentrates the discussion on the geographic centrality of the Aztec culture. This same textbook mentions only briefly the daily life of the modern Maya and omits altogether any suggestion of other cultures such as the Olmec and Zapotec.

Emerging Cultural Identity

Cultural identity lies at the heart of indigenous efforts to reclaim land and their natural and cultural resources, although indigenous rebellions in the late nineteenth century were as much about the defense of cultural and political rights as they were for land. Over the past ten years, discussions about cultural identity have become especially politicized in the Mexican state of Chiapas and in neighboring Guatemala, where indigenous groups have taken a more aggressive tone about control of their cultural identity (Fisher and Brown 1996; Goldin 1999; Hale 1997; Lovell 1990).

In Chiapas, the *Zapatista* movement (EZLN) claims to represent the direct heirs of the ancient Maya in a struggle to reclaim their heritage by gaining control over some of the natural and archaeological resources in the region. Their petitions have stressed providing access to archaeological sites and indigenous training to enable them to administer the archaeological sites themselves. They also emphasize authorizing the indigenous use of sites as ceremonial centers and protecting the sites when they are threatened by major tourist development or by looting (Muriel 2001:61).

An insurrection by Chiapas peasants in January 1, 1994, led to the deaths of 145 people and quickly attracted the attention of the world's popular press. Although the Zapatistas' social base is made up of a relatively small local following, their cause has generated sympathetic responses worldwide (van den Berghe 1995:583–584). Humanitarian support initially came from the largely mainstream international audience who responded with sympathy to the Zapatistas' demands for less political corruption and more equality and freedom for indigenous peoples. Through the actions of the Zapatistas, the world became aware of the indigenous populations in southeastern Mexico and Guatemala and with that, the realization that they could resort to violent means if they are pushed past the limits of endurance (van den Berghe 1995:585).

Occasionally, isolated Zapatista incidents continue to make news. On March 1, 2003, the *Los Angeles Times* (2003b) reported a story on the public denouncement of foreign investment in tourism projects in Mexico as Zapatista rebels stormed an American-owned ranch, brandishing machetes and driving out the ranch employees. Other recent actions involving Zapatista rebels appear to have more to do with an escalating religious conflict between Catholic and evangelical Christian groups in Chiapas than with resistance to foreign tourism investment.

As the Zapatista movement so effectively illustrates, a number of critical questions have characterized recent debates on Mexican patrimony. Many of those same questions have also been debated in the United States, especially as they relate to archaeological issues (Muriel 2001:61):

- Do ethnic groups have special rights over ancient sites, artifacts, or burials associated with their ancestry?
- Is it possible to determine definitively which group actually built some of the archaeological sites that were abandoned before the conquest?
- Are there any distinct ethnic groups remaining in Mexico after the conquest?

- How distinct were the ancient populations since people were often interacting and moving around?
- How many cultural traditions and folk memories have already been lost in the great push toward a unified Mexican culture as groups were moved to new settlement locations?

To this list, I would add these other questions: what are the significant cultural differences between the groups, and what archaeological changes can be seen through the different time periods?

The Zapatista movement successfully employs other modern approaches, most notably with the internet. They now operate a store in San Cristóbal de las Casas to sell Zapatista merchandise, and they maintain websites through which people buy products online and make donations to their cause.

Several recent and controversial proposals have called for turning Mexican archaeological zones over to private companies to operate as for-profit concessions. However, because archaeological sites are considered so integral to Mexico's national patrimony, proposals for converting them into private businesses have been consistently denied thus far.

The Ancient and Historical Maya in Quintana Roo

Before the Caste War in the mid-nineteenth century, the Maya made up almost 80 percent of the population in the Yucatán Peninsula. As commercial cultivation of sugar and henequen became the principal crops, contact between the different ethnic groups also increased, particularly in Mérida, Campeche, and Valladolid. This triggered a population shift from the colonial northwestern Yucatán to the less accessible southeastern towns of Tekax, Peto, and Tihosuco (Rugeley 2001:8–9). It is in southeastern Quintana Roo where memories of the Caste War endure as a real and vital component of Maya identity. Through ethnohistorical events and characters, the contemporary Maya see themselves as a group who continues to oppose the "Spaniards," which generally means anyone who is not Maya.

A government-promoted program of immigration further accelerated rapid shifts in population in the Yucatán Peninsula at the end of the Mexican Revolution in 1910 (Ryder 1977). In 1984, Guatemalan refugees were resettled in several areas of the Yucatán Peninsula, and the 1990 census revealed that over half the population of Quintana Roo had emigrated from elsewhere in Mexico. Over the last 30 years, the majority of emigrants have been drawn by the government's promotion of tourism development, particularly along the Maya Riviera. Today's indigenous migration generally consists of two groups: men and women who have left their villages to work in the Maya Riviera tourism business and those who have left to work in other parts of Mexico or in the United States and Canada.

As we come to understand more about Mesoamerican demography, we see a long history of group movements in and out of regions, and after the Classic Maya collapse, it now appears that people either dispersed back into the forest or sought out the emerging power centers in the lowlands of northern Quintana Roo. It may be that our modern view of land as divided into geographically defined territories of cities, states, and nations gets in the way of fully appreciating the ancient Mesoamerican worldview.

Quintana Roo in the Historical Period

After the Late Postclassic, southeastern Quintana Roo was known as a dangerous and inhospitable place to be avoided whenever possible. Little is known or recorded about the region during the seventeenth and eighteenth centuries, but there may have been a drastic drop in population, probably owing to diseases and piracy along the coast (Andrews and Andrews 1975:4; Roys 1957).

The present epoch of tourism is only the most recent period during which outsiders have sought to exploit the natural and cultural resources of Quintana Roo (Oppenheimer 1996). For centuries it was notorious as a frontier region beset by malaria and overrun by rebel guerrillas, with little consensus for how the area could next be exploited. On two occasions, in 1867 and in 1885, the Maya in Quintana Roo offered to become a formal part of the British colonial empire but were rejected both times because of British interests in other parts of Mexico. Documents suggest that at different times and in different ways, Mérida, Mexico City, and London represented the political economy of Quintana Roo, although the Maya rebels continually remained an entity to be reckoned with (Konrad 1991:143).

As sugar and logwood industries expanded in the region, foreign immigrants arrived to colonize the state lands in Quintana Roo, further contributing to the dispossession of the indigenous populations. A land rush dispossessed even more Maya after an 1843 law was passed that allowed the government to repay loans with land rather than with cash. As colonial institutions were dismantled to make way for the introduction of capitalism, the new agrarian policy was based on the widely held view that indigenous groups were intellectually backward, much as indigenous groups in the United States were viewed at around the same time.

Historian Robert Patch (1991:51) suggests that although rapid changes in agrarian laws were clearly catalysts for the start of the Caste War, such a long and destructive regional war more likely arose from a number of factors, including demographic growth. The people who carried out the new liberal agrarian policies may have genuinely believed that these laws favored the common good, although in actuality they resulted in escalating the dispossession of the Maya, as well as increasing the creole occupation of their land (Patch 1991:82).

Aguirre Beltrán (1979) called Quintana Roo a "zone of refuge" because the Maya came to this area to escape Spanish control, just as others came later to evade Mexican rule. The region then became center stage for the Caste War and the other smaller insurrections that followed (Hostettler 1997; Pi-Sunyer, Thomas, and Daltabuit 2001:125; Reed 1964; Rugeley 2001).

By the latter part of the eighteenth century, the government gave up attempts to control indigenous settlement patterns, and as those boundaries disintegrated, so did the influence of the Catholic Church and much of the enforced social cohesion (Patch 1991:58). One report noted that more than two-thirds of the Indian population had evidently moved into the bush to hide "their idolatry and to avoid paying their civil and religious taxes" (Patch 1991:59–62). During times of famine, emigration accelerated even more as communities dispersed into the thinly settled eastern and southern areas of Quintana Roo (Brannon and Joseph 1991a, b; Patch 1991:62; Reed 1964; Viliesid 1990).

Over the next 25 years, the ruling elite gradually dismantled the colonial regime in the Yucatán Peninsula, even as agrarian changes continued to limit communal property and encouraged the buying and selling of land (Brannon and Joseph 1991a, b; Patch 1991:66).

Private estates for cattle ranching and commercial agriculture became more economically and politically important in the mid-seventeenth century, where they flourished until the Mexican Revolution. The Maya could get work as laborers to tend cattle and crops, and the growth of Mérida was attractive to Maya artisans and craftsmen such as carpenters, blacksmiths, and shoemakers (Rugeley 2001:6–7). Subsistence-based communities were already realizing the necessity of a commercial aspect to their economy, and many villagers put together some sort of professional diversification.

The earliest natural resource to be exploited was logwood, but by the early 1890s the extraction of chicle had also become an important economic resource (Konrad 1991:147). When they became involved with chicle production, the *Cruzob* (The Cult of the Talking Cross) leaders were ironically faced with an inherent contradiction: while fighting for independence, they were also participating in the economy of chicle extraction, which continued the dependence they loathed.

The British began investing in Mexico immediately after its independence from Spain, primarily by building an infrastructure for communications and railroads (Konrad 1991:148–151; Villalobos 1996). Belizean woodcutters, backed by British capital, worked in the peninsula as far north as Tulum during the late 1880s and reported generally friendly relations with the Cruzob. In time, Mexican pressure to cut off the Belizean supply of goods and arms to interior towns such as Peto and Valladolid led to economic stagnation, at least until the plantation crops of sugar, tobacco, rubber, and vanilla were introduced into the area. Since the British were no longer paying rent for lumber interests, the traditional Maya subsistence activities of milpa and hunting were so compromised that the situation began to affect their social structure.

Early on, the federal government devised a strategy for national development that was guided by a group of planners called *cientificos*, who made decisions about expanding the nation's economic base beyond a reliance on the export of precious metals and agroforestry products. Since the British, through their Belizean contacts, were the only ones who had maintained a peaceful commercial relationship with the Maya rebels in Quintana Roo, the federal government eventually decided to step in. They deployed a small naval force operating out of two ports, Cozumel and the Bay of Chetumal, to prevent armaments from coming across the Belizean border and to exert more pressure on the Cruzob-held territory (Konrad 1991:152–154).

In 1898, General Ignacio Bravo was brought in to capture the Cruzob capital of Chan Santa Cruz (now called Felipe Carrillo Puerto), and after this, the victorious army was a continual presence, mainly to provide armed protection during construction of the railroad. After the railroad was completed, the area was opened up for other commercial development, although southern Quintana Roo continued to be formidable for prospective settlers due to the threat of malaria and sporadic rebel activities (Burns 1996; Konrad 1991:154–155).

In November 1902, President Porfírio Díaz officially declared Quintana Roo to be a federal territory, and economic and political control was maintained until it officially became a state in 1974. Bravo returned to serve as governor from 1903 to 1912, giving Chan Santa Cruz a commercial footing (as well as amassing his own considerable personal wealth). In 1915, a few years after Bravo had left the area, a series of negotiations between the Cruzob and Yucatec officials brought peace to the area, and before long, these same Cruzob were actively participating in the commercial development of the region (Konrad 1991:159–160).

By this time, everyone had realized that there was much to gain by developing the state of Quintana Roo: "The transformation of Quintana Roo's frontier involved an interplay of clearly identifiable interests: The local Maya's primary concern was survival and autonomy; Mérida, and to a lesser extent Campeche, wished to incorporate lost territories; Mexico City focused on a national development project and the resolution of regional separatists tendencies. The foreign capitalist stake, on the other hand, was direct access to Quintana Roo's export staples. For roughly fifty years, the only clear-cut winners were the foreign capitalists interests. Those who lost the most were the local Maya" (Konrad 1991:144). Other traditional forms of subsistence such as farming, fishing, and growing henequen had their boom-and-bust periods through the early twentieth century, but most of these strategies have now been abandoned in favor of working in the construction or tourism industries (Chacón 1991; Joseph 1991).

Nancy Farriss (1984:19) asserts, possibly with some irony, that the conquest did not really end in southeastern Quintana Roo until the death of the last of the Caste War leaders in 1969, a date that just happens to coincide with the planning stages of the tourism boom and links the end of the epoch of rebellion with the beginning of the epoch of tourism (Pi-Sunyer, Thomas, and Daltabuit 2001:125).

Memories of the Caste War

The phrase *caste war* was probably first used in a letter reporting uprisings in Teabo in April 1843. The *jefe politico* (political leader) of Ticul described it as a *guerra de castas* (caste war), although the war did not technically begin until four years later (Patch 1991:80). For Terry Rugeley (1996, 2001:11), the Caste War began as yet another planned Creole revolution aimed at garnering support from a politician named Miguel Barbachano. Although that revolt was aborted, several Maya *batabs* (village headmen or *caciques*) gradually gained a following, most notably Jacinto Pat of Tihosuco and Cecilio Chi of Tepich. In the months between July and November of 1847, the rebellion officially became known as the Caste War.

The Caste War began in 1847 and has been described as the longest and most successful Indian rebellion in the New World (Dumond 1977, 1997; Reed 1964; Sullivan 1989:xiv–xvi; Villalobos González 1996). Many contemporary Yucatec Maya proudly consider themselves the descendants of the Caste War heroes and regard the Caste War as part of God's plan for renewing the world in the "Final Days of the Era of Man" (Sullivan 1989:xvi–xix). Ancient Maya prophecies claimed that human blood must flow in order to guarantee the transition between this world and the next, and modern Cruzob see the Caste War as one of the signs that this world will soon be ending (Bricker 1977; Burns 1977).

Specific symbols are related to pivotal events during the Caste War in Quintana Roo, in much the same way that some American southerners cherish Civil War battle sites, heroes, and memorabilia. A particularly significant story of the Caste War involved the Cruzob who maintain a presence in the region as a rallying point for Maya social activism. The Caste War was such an important historical and political event in Quintana Roo that it continues to shape the response to culture change among contemporary Maya. For this reason, it is necessary to give a brief account of events leading up to the current Maya situation in Quintana Roo.

The Talking Cross (*Cruz Parlante*)

Felipe Carrillo Puerto (formerly Chan Santa Cruz) is a small town halfway between Cancún and Chetumal along federal highway 307. In the mid-nineteenth century, the town was celebrated as a theocratic entity that arose during the Caste War and was known as the place where the *Cruz Parlante* dictated religious, political, and military policy to the Maya rebels (Burns 1996; Pearce 1984:37; Reed

1964). A cult revolving around the Talking Cross began with a rebel known as José Mari Barrera. He and his fellow fighters found refuge at a small cenote that was notable because the water level never seemed to change no matter how much water was drawn from it. There was a small cross, about 4 inches in height, carved into a mahogany tree next to the cenote, and this is where legend says the cross spoke to the rebels (in a voice that resembled the voice of Manuel Nahuat, a soldier and ventriloquist). Later, Nahuat was integral in helping to launch an ill-fated skirmish in which many Maya were slaughtered, including Nahuat himself, but the phenomenon of the talking cross continues to give holy instructions through written letters (Pearce 1984:38). A chapel called La Gloria was later built at the site of the talking cross, with a pit behind the altar from which the voice of God is still said to resonate upon occasion.

Well over a century after the Caste War, Maya counsels continued to stress the importance of the power of "the cross" for instructing society. For the Maya there are no clear distinctions between what happens because of fate and what happens because of human intervention, helping to explain, at least in part, the enduring belief in the talking cross.

The Link Between Modern and Ancient Maya

Is there a discernible association in Quintana Roo between the ancient and modern Maya in the public consciousness? In my view, the enduring aura of the Maya offers one of the most compelling stories to be told about the region. Developers and tourism officials use Mayan words and images to appeal to tourists, but there is little else in the commercial world that recognizes the Maya as a viable modern presence in the Maya Riviera. Once, a woman who volunteers for a missionary program in the United States told me that although she had been coming to Quintana Roo for more than ten years, she had yet to actually meet a Maya. She was startled to learn that Maya workers were all around her, and indeed they had been cleaning her hotel rooms and serving her food throughout her annual visits to Cancún.

Today, there are more than one million modern Maya living in the Yucatán Peninsula, although they are often overlooked by the public's enthusiasm for their romanticized ancestors (Andrews 1965; Dufresne 1999; Marín and Gubler 1997; Pfeiler 1997; Restall 1997; Watanabe 1995:25). As with the mound builders of North America, early explorers to Mexico were hard-pressed to make the connection between the mysterious ruins of a once majestic civilization and the impoverished Indians they encountered. Even though explorer John Lloyd Stephens was one of the first to argue that the ruined cities had been built by the ancestors of the contemporary Maya, his books, *Incidents of Travel in Central America, Chiapas, and Yucatan* (1841) and *Incidents of Travel in the Yucatan* (1843) helped to create the image of an enigmatic, lost civilization that stirred the public imagination and were best-sellers when they first came out.

Actually, the continual presence of the modern Maya distinguishes the region from many other parts of the world where the indigenous populations have completely disappeared and provides an admittedly tenuous link with the region's long-abandoned Maya cities (Bartolomé n.d.; Brown 1996, 1999; Hostettler 2001; Penalosa 1996). The modern Maya are often a shadowy presence for visitors, especially at archaeological sites, where tourism officials and guides have been slow to make use of the connection.

Archaeologists have come to realize that the local workers they hire to work on excavations occasionally have bits and pieces of religious, calendrical, and cultural knowledge connecting them to the ancient Maya. There are limitations of course, and some would argue that it can be problematic when archaeologists use Maya ethnographies to project beliefs and behaviors that are observed in the ethnographic present back to the time of the ancient Maya (Fedick 2003; Gifford 1978a; Howry 1978).

There are many reasons for why most visitors find it difficult to envisage a clear connection between the ancient and modern Maya. Geographically, most of the large monumental structures are situated in isolated locations or in established parks, leading visitors to infer that the people who built them have long since disappeared. This is the case with most other once-great civilizations, such as the Minoans of ancient Crete and the Moche of Peru.

Fundamental differences between the approaches of Maya archaeologists and anthropologists working with the modern Maya have also contributed to misconceptions (Pearce 1984:xi–xii). In general, archaeologists have tended to focus on elite activities in the ancient ceremonial centers, while anthropologists have focused their efforts primarily upon cultural patterns among modern peasants. These quite different approaches are often dictated by circumstance, but they also perpetuate the notion that the magnificent powerful past belongs exclusively to a long-gone civilization (Pearce 1984:xii). Archaeologists may be contributing further to the ancient/modern disjuncture by using nineteenth-century names that reinforce the notion that the buildings are abandoned wreckage, such as Ruined House (*Labná*), Ruined Wall (*Xlappahk*), Fragment of Head (*Xethpol*), and Low Wall (*Cabalpak*) (Pearce 1984:6).

Notably, one of the most substantial links between the ancient and modern Maya is found in the retention of the Yucatec Mayan language. Today, Yucatec Mayan ranks as the second largest indigenous language spoken in Mexico (after Nahuatl), and the number of Yucatec Mayan speakers has actually increased over the last 50 years (Rugeley 2001:199).

A visitor to Cancún's Tourist Zone is met by an array of confusing messages about the modern Maya and their ancient cultural heritage. A winding road leads into the *Zona Turista* (Tourist Zone), passing giant sculptures of Olmec heads, Aztec calendars, and other Caribbean (as opposed to Mexican) representations, positioned along the landscaped median. The architecture and room decor at the hotels blend Maya themes with those of other ethnic groups in a confusing array, almost as if a cultural void had to be filled quickly with whatever was available. Anthropologist Alicia Re Cruz (1996:145) described her first reaction to Cancún when she was struck by the stereotyping of both the ancient and modern Maya as "museum pieces," as, for example, traditionally dressed Maya women making tortillas or waiting on tables in the restaurants. "Given this Disneyland-like version of the archaeological past, foreign guests commonly believe that the Maya are 'extinct'" (Pi-Sunyer, Thomas, and Daltabuit 2001:130).

7 Public Interpretation at Mexican Museums

Mexican museums have been especially influential in creating a national identity, and one of the ways they have done this has been through the promotion of local artisan production of arts and crafts. Whenever artisans are encouraged to re-create older designs as part of their modern craft production, they are also functioning as repositories for collecting, conserving, and interpreting the symbols of their cultural heritage (Blundell 1993; Cone 1995; Hobgood and Riley 1978; Kaplan 1993:103–104; Moreno and Littrell 2001).

After the revolution in 1910, Manuel Gamio's (1960) quest for a national identity resulted in a cultural campaign to unite all Mexicans by emphasizing cultural patrimony. This quest gave additional value to the artistic expressions of folk art and folklore because Mexican museums in the late eighteenth and early nineteenth centuries were part of a system that supported the growth of nationalism and the formation of the modern state (Kaplan 1993:104).

In eighteenth-century Mexico, the archaeological excavations and museum exhibits fed the public's enthusiasm for its past civilizations. A colonial governor named Viceroy Bucareli collected the famous *Coatlicue* sculpture and the Aztec Calendar Stone, and placed them among other treasures at a university. By the early nineteenth century, the first official archaeological museum was founded with the objective of presenting past and present Mexican civilizations as accurately as possible. To accomplish this goal, artists and traditional materials were brought in from all over the country to encourage indigenous involvement in the museum's design (Kaplan 1993:105–113).

The Mexican government also promoted the preservation of traditional folklore and crafts through various museum exhibitions, publications, and other activities. In order to sell crafts in museum shops and outlets, modern artists have learned to reproduce ancient artifacts and design new ones, although these crafts have become increasingly commercialized over the years. Presently, there are over 50 indigenous institutions and agencies at work to promote popular art in Mexico; the most prominent include Instituto Nacional Indigenista (INI), Fideicomiso para el Fomento del Las Artesanías (now the BANFOCO), Secretaria de Trabajadores no Asalariados y Artesanos de La CNOP, and Instituto Mexicano de Comércio Exterior (IMCE).

Some critics decry all museums as representing at best only a partial picture of the past, thereby legitimizing the perspectives of the dominant elite (Merriman 2000; Thomas 2002). If the role of museums is to impart some idea of "what happened in history," then it is fair to question the objective and subjective approaches to museum displays. Museums generally aim to tell noteworthy stories about the past, despite the fact that they have not been all that successful in suggesting multiple divergent perspectives. An important early step toward multiple interpretations would oblige museums to function not only as places where stories are told but also as places where people can evaluate the evidence for themselves (Merriman 2000:303–305).

Presenting separate versions of the same story, or "multivocalism," reflects a particularly important trend in museum experience (Stone 1997, Tufts and Milne 1999). Rather than relying on a pre-set monologue, some museums are developing more dynamic strategies for dialogue with visitors, who are then encouraged to form their own personal opinions. This is well expressed by Merriman: "A display of classical sculptures in Britain will mean something quite different to a similar display in Greece, and all will be interpreted quite differently by Greeks in Greece, Greeks living in Britain, British tourists in Greece, and British people in Britain" (2000:304–305).

The potential utility of multivocalism is demonstrated by the multiple stories that could possibly be told to visitors to the Alamo (Thomas 2002:134–142). Most U.S. history texts describe it as a heroic episode in the Texas War of Independence against Mexico, although closer scrutiny suggests that Mexicans have been excluded from any sort of honorable role in this integral part of official Texas history. Some archaeologists have proposed conducting further excavations for a more complete picture of the battle at the Alamo. However, the Daughters of the Republic of Texas, the state-appointed custodians of the Alamo and its archaeological record, claim that this research would detract from the true historical significance of the site, now known as the "thirteen days of glory." As David Hurst Thomas (2002:36) explained, recognizing the historical significance of the earlier mission period and honoring the Mexican soldiers would threaten the current sociopolitical power in modern San Antonio, despite the fact that tourists to the Alamo put the archaeologists under considerable pressure to do so.

Because Hispanics now make up a third of the population of Texas, public school textbooks have been revised to present a more balanced view of the events at the Alamo. Many feel that it is crucial to present the points of view from both sides of the conflict, "even if that means soft-pedaling the fact that the historical battle largely pitted one ethnic group against another" (Cieply and Eller 2003:A12). Notably, it is rarely acknowledged that the American defenders of the Alamo were called the *rebeldes esclavistas* by their Mexican foes because they were fighting to retain their slaves, while Mexico had by then abolished slavery.

Margaret Mead once sagely remarked that museums have held the steadfast trust of the public primarily because they ask "Is it true?" instead of "Will this be a hit?" (Thomas 2002:143–144). Museums should provide a forum for public debate (Merriman 2000:306), and when an exhibit is linked to current issues, such as problems with the environment, demographics, or city planning, the public is more likely to see the displays as relevant and inspiring. By incorporating contemporary issues, museums have the potential to promote constructive dialogues on issues that matter in the real world.

Embracing multivocal displays means that museums need to state explicitly the agenda of an exhibition and encourage visitors to accept or reject it (Merriman 2000:307). Perhaps more than anything else, a good balance is needed between the archaeological interpretation and collaboration with indigenous peoples and interest groups. An interdisciplinary approach is also useful for achieving the most relevant information across traditional geographical and subject boundaries (P. Davis 2000:317, Horne 1984; Kaplan 1993; Tufts and Milne 1999).

Museums have a tendency to present the past as if there were only one reality, even though there are often several alternative perspectives involved. It may be that museums and archaeological parks will eventually evolve into places where people are able to evaluate the evidence critically while viewing the presentations (Merriman 2000:303; Smardz 1997).

My research on the public interpretation in Quintana Roo included all of the museums that represent archaeology and culture. They ranged from the popular and respected Museum of the Maya Culture in Chetumal to the Tihosuco-based Museum of the Caste War, which rarely receives non-Maya visitors. To gain a larger perspective, I also explored museums in the states of Yucatán and Chiapas, primarily because they are well known for their educational approaches.

INAH Cancún Museum, Quintana Roo

The INAH Cancún Museum is tucked away in an unobtrusive corner of an older outdoor shopping and business mall that once served as the Convention Center. Since a newer and grander, not to mention enclosed and air-conditioned, Convention Center and shopping mall have been built, this particular area no longer attracts many tourists. The museum and the old convention center area have been scheduled for extensive renovation but for now sit forlornly with mostly empty offices and shops. Without specific directions, it is likely the average visitor to Cancún would be more apt to think it is a business office than a public museum.

Relatively early in Cancún's development, FONATUR (the agency charged with tourism development in Mexico) donated the building to INAH for conversion into a museum and personnel offices (FONATUR n.d.). There was pressure to open the museum within a very short period of time, so the building was hastily renovated to result in the current floor plan. There were plans for expanding and renovating the museum until 1986, when Hurricane Gilberto destroyed the museum, so it was closed to repair the damage. In 1995, it reopened in the same location after the building was reconstructed, but less than ideal building materials were used, and directional and educational signage was not considered a high priority. Although the museum receives some funds each month for maintenance and new annual projects, it doesn't allow much for signage, advertising, or other forms of public interpretation. Although FONATUR maintains responsibility for all tourism signage, the agency has provided only a minimal number of signs for INAH venues. Museum officials report that relatively few Americans visit the museum, and most visitors come from Canada, Europe, and Asia. They have usually read about the museum in a guidebook and come to see the artifacts on display and browse in the small gift shop.

The INAH Cancún Museum functions with very limited financial options; for example, the gift shop must return the proceeds from all sales to the national INAH headquarters, even though the salaries of salesclerks and other staff members are directly paid by the museum. At present, there is a trend toward hiring professionally trained administrators for top INAH positions rather than the earlier pattern of hiring trained archaeologists and promoting them to administrative positions. There is little job security at the administrative levels, and officials work without contracts and can be relocated at any time without explanation. The INAH Cancún Museum maintains a staff of four daytime guards, two ticket sellers, and three nighttime guards, but this list does not include all of the job categories or expenses for mandatory 24-hour shifts, sick leave, and vacations. Other than the administrators, the employees are unionized, so they currently enjoy more job security and benefits than their supervisors. With union backing, staff members cannot be required to work "an extra minute" or perform duties outside their contract specifications (personal communication August 2002).

Museum of the Maya Culture—Chetumal, Quintana Roo

The governor of Quintana Roo built this informative and accessible museum in 1993 as part of a statewide improvement plan. There was a tough debate on whether to build the museum in Cancún, where most tourists are likely to visit, or in Chetumal, the state's capital that was badly in need of some cultural development. In the end, it was built in Chetumal, and it manages to attract large numbers of visitors, mostly made up of school groups and those who come because of strong recommendations in tourist guidebooks. This museum is not INAH operated, although it was built with the cooperation of INAH experts. Almost all of the exhibited artifacts are actually replicas, which the museum makes up for by offering visitors an exceptional number of well-designed multimedia and interactive presentations on the region's geography, cultural history, and biodiversity. In addition, the museum offers in-depth information on Maya writing, mythology, and calendar systems. Somewhat oddly, much of the information relates to Classic Period Maya sites even though, other than Cobá, most archaeological sites in Quintana Roo were built in the Postclassic.

Archaeological and cultural information is presented within a tropical forest background featuring large artificial trees, vines, and flowers. Continual sounds of howler monkeys, exotic birds, and rainfall are meant to be reminiscent of the primeval forest. At one point, the visitor comes upon scale models of some of the most famous Maya archaeological sites, although this display is set into the floor under glass so visitors get a bird's-eye perspective as they walk over them.

Museum of the Maya People—Dzibilchaltun, Yucatán

Designed to provide an overview of the Maya culture, the INAH-operated museum offers a perspective on the regional colonial period as well as the history of the archaeological site of Dzibilchaltun. The museum has two buildings, one dedicated to the archaeological materials excavated from the site itself and the other relating to the historical era through the conquest and colonial periods. An exhibit of altars and religious paraphernalia effectively demonstrates the syncretism of Maya prehistoric and early Christian beliefs. One particular exhibit emphasizes how the Maya carefully recorded colonial-era events in papers, letters, and drawings, demonstrating the "florid memories" of lineages, counts of time, and the harrowing violence of the conquest—all with a touch of melancholy for the ways of the world.

In another section of the museum, the visitor walks across a floor laid with glass panels where, through tricks of lighting, it seems as if the visitor is gazing at several underwater shipwrecks ranging from ancient Maya canoes of traders to ships from the colonial period.

This museum is special at least in part because it presents the Maya point of view, together with an air of sad resignation that such events have come to pass. The goal was to put poetic expression to the suffering and devastation the Maya have endured. The words represent a political message unvarnished by political correctness, even though it does not condemn anyone other than the Spanish, who conquered, then colonized the region. Throughout the museum, various messages express a particular political point of view rather than attempt a straight recitation of facts. At this museum, the focus is on the poignancy of the Maya response and long-term resilience, with all that implies. The museum explicitly attempts to convey the bond that unites all modern Maya with the traditions of their ancestors and has a point of view that is rarely heard elsewhere.

Figure 18. Museum of the Caste War, Tihosuco, Quintana Roo

Museum of the Caste War—Tihosuco, Quintana Roo

The descriptions on the walls of this museum (not INAH operated) represent the long-held Maya hope of regaining their liberty and returning to their social organization from before the Conquest (Figure 18). This perspective presents Spanish domination and intention to turn indigenous peoples into submissive, depersonalized beings by detaching them from their history and subduing them physically and spiritually. Faced with the reality, the Maya sought solace by preserving their own languages and religion and by maintaining the milpa tradition, all of which helped to sustain Maya unity and identity. This exhibit makes it easier to understand how "the Caste War arose from mythic origins fueled by desires for a future offering liberty, justice and rights to land" (sign on museum wall, April 2003).

Tihosuco, an inland town of about 7,000 people, was chosen to be home to this museum when it was commissioned by the governor of Quintana Roo in 1993. Since it is well off the tourist path, it receives only about 300 to 400 visitors a year, mostly Maya and other ethnic Mexican school groups. Museum employees claim they would ideally like to have perhaps between 50 and 100 visitors a day to the museum and the community. This area lacks all of the usual tourist lures of beaches and luxury hotels, and even the archaeological sites of Chichén Itzá and Tulum are far away. Ironically, most of the Maya in this area have never visited these great archaeological sites because they live too far and don't have enough money to travel. They cannot afford to visit the theme parks of Xcaret or Xel Há either, so they have no real opinion about how their heritage is being represented at such venues (personal communication, April 2003).

As yet, there is not even a restaurant, much less a hotel or other visitor services in Tihosuco, although they are considering putting together a cooperative association to build a place for visitors to eat and relax. They stress that they don't want to encourage the type of mass tourism found in Cancún, although they welcome the more focused tourists who want to learn about traditional food, herbs, crafts, and the Mayan language (personal communication, April 2003). In the past, tourists in this region were not always welcomed as they were regarded as part of the Spanish colonization; however, the residents of Tihosuco have come to enjoy the tourists who have visited out of historical or scientific interest, as well as the money they spend in town. Most of the homes in Tihosuco now have televisions, but to make money, many adults have to leave for weeks at a time to work in Playa del Carmen, Xcaret, or Cancún. When asked if this arrangement is seen as harmful to Maya families, I was told that they generally become accustomed to this routine and report few problems (personal communication, April 2003).

It is obvious that this museum serves a positive role in the town as a social center and important resource for teaching and other social activities. Six people are currently employed by the museum, ranging from the *ecargado,* or director, a teacher, a promotion coordinator, guards, and cleaning attendants. There is a support group, called the *Amigos de Museo* (Friends of the Museum), who preserve and disperse information about such things as traditional folk medicine, local history, and the Maya calendrical system.

After spending most of the day at the museum, it was evident that it is a source of great pride for the community and serves as a meeting place for children for after-school programs on crafts and Maya history classes. It also functions as a place for adults to socialize on an informal basis. There is a garden with traditional Maya plants and a small area with local arts and crafts for sale, but most important, there is a genuine sense of community at this museum.

A few of the signs had been translated into English a year earlier, although most of the text is only in Spanish and Yucatec Mayan. Translating into English is a time-consuming task, and much of the text is so poetic that it is difficult to translate into another language, as demonstrated by this short section: "When the yellow wind swept the sky; the prophetic stones speak of harvest."

The primary objective of the museum is to provide the Maya point of view in the Mayan language, so a group of Maya descendants were closely involved in all of the planning and building stages. In scope, this is an intimate museum, although the perspective does not ignore the impact of historical events that happened elsewhere, such as a portion of text detailing Mexico's loss of the territory of Texas and the North American intervention in 1847 and its influence on the short-lived independence of the Yucatán Peninsula. The Maya version of the Caste War places emphasis on the Maya potential rather than criticizing Spanish colonialism. As an example, Fra Diego de Landa is described as a complex man who, while dedicated to recording the Maya traditions for posterity, at the same time practiced racism and religious intolerance toward the Maya people.

For this Maya community, it is crucial to understand and remember all that happened during the Caste War because they see war as the cause of great suffering. Maya visitors see their own reflections in the museum's stories, and present-day tensions make it a story well worth repeating. The message taken away is that these Maya, while informed by the past, are looking forward toward a better future, which they hope to be able to choose for themselves.

Representations of Authenticity

For visitors and host communities the concepts of "authentic" and "sustainable" mean different things. Tourists are seldom able to experience authentic cultural events because traditional events rapidly become commercialized as they are made available to tourists (MacCannell 1976). Tourists are usually attracted to the events that are popular within the host community and often enjoy the event even if its authenticity is in doubt. Quetzil Castaneda (1996:104–105) has argued that because archaeological investigations involve destructive processes, an uncontested authenticity is an unrealistic concept under any circumstances. None of this matters anyway because the public will accept it as long as there is no transparent contradiction of the popular criteria for authenticity.

The principle of authenticity drives much of the contemporary heritage industry and can be applied to museums, historic homes, national parks, archaeological excavations, and even towns (McManamon and Hatton 2000:1). Particularly since World War II, the United States has held the concept of authenticity as a central part of cultural resource management (CRM) and heritage management. Authenticity remains an integral part of the debate on heritage within the disciplines of archaeology, anthropology, museum management, and conservation (Jameson 1997, 2000; Kwas 2000; Kwas and Mainfort 1996; Lerner and Hoffman 2000; McManamon 2000a, b).

Whenever the U.S. National Park Service performs conservation work on structures, it is now based on an accurate duplication of documented features rather than on conjectural designs (De Bloois and Schneider 1989; Jameson and Hunt 1999). Whenever possible, conservation takes place on the original site and at full scale to suggest the appearance of nonsurviving parts of buildings in terms of design, color, textures, and materials. To be truly effective, archaeological interpretation needs to find a way to stimulate an intellectual and emotional connection (Getz 1994:322–323; Uzzell 1989:46).

Donald Getz (1994:315) claims that the term *authentic* implies that it is the real thing and carries two connotations: tourists seldom get access to authentic cultural experiences, and the tourist demand tends to undermine traditional culture anyway. On the other hand, heritage events can be useful interpretive tools to reveal the values, traditions, and sense of place within a community. Heritage events also reveal interrelationships between social groups, or even between people and the environment, especially when they provide an opportunity for tourist interaction with sites, objects, and re-created ways of life.

Weighing Site Preservation with Visitor Access

While building the Parc Pyrénéen d'Art Préhistorique in the French Pyrenees, Jean Clottes and Christopher Chippendale (1999:194–205) were able to define several important factors for protecting the environment of an ancient site while making it more accessible and effective in public interpretation. The problems involved with maintaining access and meeting the public demand at the French Paleolithic painted cave of Niaux led to the creation of an innovative park at the site. In earlier years, public demand had dictated access to the cave until its popularity grew to such an extent that it became necessary to determine the sustainability of the cave's environment and restrict access accordingly. At the present time, it is considered to be more critical to determine the maximum human capacity at a cave such as Niaux than to provide access to all of the visitors who want to visit. While the authors (1999:195) admit that a maximum carrying capacity is difficult to define precisely, they argue that it can be effectively estimated. Niaux Cave is now carefully monitored for temperature, humidity, and other data for identifying the optimal carrying capacity. When there are any negative indicators, the numbers of visitors are immediately curtailed.

On any given day, a maximum number of 220 individuals may visit Niaux cave. However, the daily number of visitors who want to view Niaux is many times higher than that number, so it was necessary to find alternatives to letting everyone in or turning away large numbers of visitors. As the official tourism season lengthens and the numbers of potential visitors grows larger every year, so do the increasingly conflicting needs of preserving Niaux cave while providing visitor access. Officials decided to follow the successful model at Lascaux, where a re-creation called Lascaux II had been exactingly replicated with identically colored images rendered on the same types of surfaces as in the original cave.

Visitor questionnaires at Niaux II currently report a 90 percent satisfaction rating, likely because the park has effectively addressed some of the more fundamental interpretive issues. However, the authors also point out that any reconstructions and reenactments will never be completely understood because visitors to the Stone

Age cave arrive with their twenty-first-century mentality and can only make sense of the site by relating the experience to elements they know directly (Clottes and Chippendale 1999:194–205).

Studying the forces behind culture change is important for anthropologists, but some question whether anything in a culture is ever *not* staged, since all cultures "are in the process of 'making themselves up' all the time" (Crick 1989:336; Greenwood 1982, 1989; Hashimoto 2000). The definitions of authenticity, or more precisely the factors we use to determine authenticity, have long been debated without coming to much of a consensus. For my research, "authentic" has meant that it was present in the past. For instance, if an architectural feature is excavated but not restored, it is authentic because it was built and used in the past. If it has been modified or conserved in modern times, then it retains some portion of authenticity but has other elements as well.

Authenticity may actually be a self-destroying process when the popularity of a site or event gradually renders it less and less authentic (*Los Angeles Times* 2003a; van den Berghe 1994:9). Some studies indicate that tourism promotes conservation measures and encourages the maintenance of traditions, while others suggest that tourism more often damages the very environment it promotes (Crick 1989:337; Price 2000). Likewise, some research specifies that there is a positive contribution because at least some money is distributed within the local community, yet other studies suggest that tourism money inevitably ends up in the pockets of investors. A similar dichotomy exists within cultural studies where for every report on tourism's role in weakening cultural traditions, there are other indicators that tourism raises awareness of the need to preserve cultural traditions (Cohen 1978; Crick 1989:337; Graburn 1983). It is not really surprising that tourism has so many dissimilar and complex effects, but as with all research, neither should we be surprised by the influences of the researchers' personal values.

8 Conclusion

Oh! Let us grieve for they have arrived from the East they came, the bearded
men, the strangers from the land, the blonde men arrived in these lands!
(sign on the wall of the stairwell in the Museo de
la Cultura Maya, Chetumal, Quintana Roo)

These words convey a foreboding about the arrival of the Spanish conquistadors, but they might also express the viewpoint of today's Maya who are engulfed by tourism. Without doubt, the state of Quintana Roo continues to undergo unprecedented and radical changes as more and more land is converted into luxury hotels, gas stations, and tourist attractions.

Neocolonial is a term sometimes used to portray the existing forms of cultural, economic, and political interaction between developed and developing nations (Nash 1989:38–40; Smith 1989:8). The continuous onslaught of new arrivals acts as a colonizing influence that threatens the traditional Maya lifestyle. Outlined here are some basic conclusions derived from my research over the past several years. These conclusions are meant for any reader, scholar, or layman who shares an interest in Mexico, the ancient and modern Maya, and the archaeology and culture of the Maya Riviera.

There are at least two distinct themes of discourse on tourism development along the Maya Riviera, and they are separated roughly into those who make a living from tourism and those who object to the way things are being done in the region. People who work in the tourism industry naturally hope it will continue to flourish, whether the informant is Mexican, Maya, or an expatriate from the United States or Europe. Those who hold the other perspective express a growing concern about the current rate of development and would like to see it moderated and implemented with more judicious attention paid to social and environmental regulations.

Other forms of activism are driven by reactions to proposals by locals who hope to change particular neighborhoods or towns. Informal activism may take the benign form of initiating a weekly Sunday afternoon beach cleanup campaign. Or may be a more organized and impassioned activism as demonstrated by a 2002 incident in Playa del Carmen where about 500 workers from Chiapas were arrested for squatting on city-owned land. Federal charges were quickly dismissed, but the city fined each squatter 35,000 pesos (about $3,500), which of course they could not pay. Eventually, local activists were able to get all of the charges dismissed, but it was a big deal in the area and has generated a lot of debate. Environmental and social activists are not yet strongly organized or working effectively together, but there are a few signs that the activist spirit is gaining momentum in the Maya Riviera, much as it is in other parts of the world.

The Maya response to the process of modernization is characterized by both adaptation and resistance, above all when it follows on the heels of tourism development (Juárez 2002:119–120; Pi-Sunyer, Thomas, and Daltabuit 2001:126). How a people respond generally depends on their life circumstances, and it varies from villagers who maintain a largely traditional lifestyle in a rural Maya community to those who have fully moved into the modern world of Cancún and Playa del Carmen. Most of the Maya informants I interviewed recognize that they are attempting to navigate between the two worlds with differing degrees of success. Workers earning only about $10 a day realize they are being exploited, but they no longer see going back to subsistence agriculture as a viable alternative. When Maya respondents were asked whether things would be better if there were no tourism, 78 percent responded that it would not be better, suggesting that while there is a nostalgia for the past and a concern for the loss of Maya identity and language, many Maya still think that working in the tourism industry offers them the best opportunity to rise out of the deeper levels of poverty (Pi-Sunyer, Thomas, and Daltabuit 2001:126–130).

Other social and political issues, such as the excavation of ancient Maya burials, are already heavily debated in the United States and have the potential to also become controversial in Quintana Roo. At present, there are hints of a budding Maya sense of patrimony, but for now it remains in the background. That said, it would be prudent for officials to recognize the well-documented, deeply independent nature of the Yucatec Maya, for whom the Caste War remains such a source of pride. As more people immigrate into the Yucatán Peninsula to find work, population pressures could once again stimulate that rebellious spirit as local sociopolitical and economic problems intensify.

A better understanding of the issues could provide meaningful solutions for problems, but an elitist bias against tourism studies often gets in the way, at least on occasion. The study of cultural tourism attempts to explain one culture to people from other cultures, as does the discipline of anthropology, and we should not be content with declaring that anthropology is a good thing because it represents scholarship, and tourism is a bad thing because it represents the exchange of money.

It is no longer sufficient merely to study social problems under the umbrella of social science research. Research findings must now be *applied* to find solutions for those social problems, and it is incumbent upon anthropologists to employ their hard-gained understanding toward making the world a better place. As recommended by June Nash (2001:219–220), anthropologists must go beyond the task of salvaging waning traditions to reporting from the frontiers of global integration.

Applied anthropology is a term for employing anthropological principles to find remedies for real-life problems, but any application requires a careful consideration of the biological, linguistic, and cultural problems inherent in the situation (Pyburn and Wilk 2000). Although my research began with the goal of exploring the ways that visitors are educated about ancient Maya archaeological sites in the Maya Riviera, it gradually evolved to a consideration of how tourism development has affected (some would say overwhelmed) the social, economic, and environmental circumstances in the region. The Maya Riviera is tailor-made for researchers to apply anthropological principles for finding solutions for real-world local problems. As Erve Chambers (1997:2) suggests, it is the precarious space between condemning the consequences and understanding the pervasiveness of tourism that holds the most promise for anthropological discussion.

This book has considered the potential benefits and apparent drawbacks associated with tourism development in the Maya Riviera from the perspectives of both scholarly research and applied anthropology. The following recommendations are directed toward any readers, whether fellow academics, tourism officials, or those with a special interest in the Maya Riviera. These recommendations are concerned with some of the more pressing regional issues and are based upon my best understanding of the past and present state of affairs. They include:

- Re-evaluate the overall tourism plan for the Maya Riviera, keeping in mind that there is nothing inherently wrong with tourism, but the need for sustainability is a factor that can no longer be ignored.
- Enact stricter laws and regulations while encouraging more effective enforcement since the region will surely continue to deteriorate without them.
- Find ways for local communities to become involved and pay close attention to local problems.
- Offer effective public oversight and enforcement through more vigilant watchdog groups and greater responsibility in media reports.
- Pay more attention to producing a high-quality tourism experience, especially as it applies to heritage and archaeological sites.
- Provide better training opportunities in business management for aspiring entrepreneurs, especially those from the poorest sectors.
- Listen to experts on environmental and social issues to learn about the problems and potential solutions.
- Devise a plan for INAH to receive greater financial aid from city and state governments that allows for more effective conservation and educational materials, especially to the most heavily impacted archaeological sites, as has been done in other Mexican states.
- Encourage more anthropological research, particularly as applied to anthropology projects, to help bring about tangible improvements to this still beautiful region.

Bibliography

Adelson, N. (2000). *El Mundo Maya sin Mayas.* Electronic document, http:/fwww.jornada. unam.mx/mas-mayas.html (accessed December 12, 2000).

Alarcón, D. C. (1997). *The Aztec Palimpsest Mexico in Modern Imagination.* Tucson, University of Arizona Press.

Anderson, E. N. (2001). In *Traditional Knowledge of Plant Resources. Lowland Maya Area: Three Millennia at the Human-Wildlife Interface,* University of California, Riverside.

Andrews, A. P., and Robert Corletta (1995). "A Brief History of Underwater Archaeology in the Maya Area." *Ancient Mesoamerica* 6:101–107.

Andrews, E. W. IV (1965). Archaeology and Prehistory in the Northern Maya Lowlands. In *Handbook of Middle American Indians,* R. Wauchope, ed., 288–330. Austin, University of Texas Press.

Andrews, E. W. IV, and Anthony P. Andrews (1975). *A Preliminary Study of the Ruins of Xcaret, Quintana Roo, Mexico with Notes on Other Archaeological Remains on the Central East Coast of the Yucatan Peninsula.* New Orleans, Middle American Research Institute, Tulane University.

Arden, T. (2002). "Conversations about the Production of Archaeological Knowledge and Community Museums at Chunchucmil and Kochol, Yucatan, Mexico." *World Archaeology* 34, 2, Community Archaeology 379–400.

Avila, A. (1995). In *Escuela Nacional de Antropologia e Historia, INAH una Historia.* C. Olive Negrete, ed., Mexico City, INAH-CENCA, 211–328.

Bartolomé, M. A. (n.d.). *La Dinamica Social de los Mavas de Yucatan Pasado y Presente de Ia Situacion Colonial.* Mexico City, Instituto Nacional Indigenista.

Batisse, M. (1982). "The Biosphere Reserve: A Tool for Environmental Conservation and Management." *Environmental Conservation* 9(2):101–110.

Beltrán, A. (1979). *Regions of Refuge.* Washington, D.C., Society for Applied Anthropology.

Beltrán, E., and Mariano Rojas (1996). "Diversified Funding Methods in Mexican Archaeology." *Annals of Tourism Research* 23(2):463–478.

Beyette, B. (2003). "The Cancuning of Cabo." *Los Angeles Times,* March 2, L1–4.

Blundell, V. (1993). "Aboriginal Empowerment and the Souvenir Trade." *Annals of Tourism Research* 20:64–87.

Bodley, J. H. (2001). *Anthropology and Contemporary Human Problems.* Mountain View, Calif., and London, Mayfield Publishing Co.

Bosselman, F. P., Craig A. Peterson, and Claire McCarthy (1999). *Managing Tourism Growth: Issues and Applications.* Washington, D.C., Island Press.

Brannon, J. T. (1991). Conclusion: Yucatecan Political Economy in Broader Perspective.

In *Land, Labor, and Capital in Modern Yucatán: Essays in Regional History and Political Economy,* J. T. Brannon, and Gilbert M. Joseph, eds., 243–250. Tuscaloosa and London, The University of Alabama Press.

Brannon, J. T., and Gilbert M. Joseph, eds. (1991a). *Land, Labor, and Capital in Modern Yucatán: Essays in Regional History and Political Economy.* Tuscaloosa and London, The University of Alabama Press.

Brannon, J. T., and Gilbert M. Joseph (1991b). The Erosion of Traditional Society: The Early Expansion of Commercial Agriculture and the Mayan Response. In *Land, Labor, and Capital in Modern Yucatán: Essays in Regional History and Political Economy,* J. T. Brannon and Gilbert M. Joseph, eds., 13–17. Tuscaloosa and London, The University of Alabama Press.

Brannon, J. T., and Gilbert M. Joseph (1991c). Revolutionary Challenges to the Plantation Regime. In *Land, Labor, and Capital in Modern Yucatán: Essays in Regional History and Political Economy,* J. T. Brannon, and Gilbert M. Joseph, eds., 175–178. Tuscaloosa and London, The University of Alabama Press.

Bricker, V. R. (1977). The Caste War of Yucatán: The History of a Myth and the Myth of History. In *Anthropology and History in Yucatán,* G. D. Jones, ed., 251–258. Austin and London, University of Texas Press.

Britton, R. A. (1979). "The Image of the Third World in Tourism Marketing." *Annals of Tourism Research* 6:318–328.

Brohman, J. (1993). Directions in Tourism for Third World Development. *Annals of Tourism Research* 23(1):48–70.

Brown, D. F. (1996). La Organizacion Social y Espacial de Ciudades Mayas: Aportaciones de Ia Antropologia Social. In *Los Mayas de Quintana Roo,* U. Hostettler, ed. Bern, Instituts fur Ethnologie der Universitat Bern.

Brown, D. F. (1999). Mayas and Tourists in the Maya World. *Human Organization* 58(3): 295–304.

Burns, A. F. (1977). The Caste War in the 1970's: Present-Day Accounts from Village Quintana Roo. In *Anthropology and History in Yucatán,* G. D. Jones, ed., 259–274. Austin and London, University of Texas Press.

Burns, A. F. (1996). Diálogos y Metáforas en Los Consejos Historicos Orales de Los "Santa Cruz Maya" de Quintana Roo. In *Los Mayas de Quintana Roo,* 41–46. Bern, Instituts fur Ethnologie der Universitat Bern.

Burns, P. M. (1999). *An Introduction to Tourism and Anthropology.* London and New York, Routledge.

Call, W. (2001). Lines in the Sand: A Tourism Debacle in Southern Mexico. Dollars & Sense, The Riviera Maya. Electronic Document, November–December 2001 (accessed July 2002).

Cancun Tips (2001a). The Riviera Maya. *Cancun Tips Magazine* 31.

Cancun Tips (2001b). Xel Ha Xel Ha Xel Ha. *Cancun Tips Magazine* 36.

Castaneda, Q. (1996). *In the Museum of Maya Culture.* Minneapolis, University of Minnesota Press.

Ceniceros, J. A. (1962). *Glosas Constitucionales. Historicas y Educativas.* Mexico City, Atisbos.

Chacón, R. D. (1991). Salvador Alvarado and Agrarian Reform in Yucatán, 1915–1918: Federal Obstruction of Regional Social Change. In *Land, Labor, and Capital in Modern Yucatán, Essays in Regional History and Political Economy*, J. T.Brannon and Gilbert M. Joseph, eds., 179–196. Tuscaloosa and London, The University of Alabama Press.

Chambers, E., ed. (1997). *Tourism and Culture—An Applied Perspective*. Albany, State University of New York.

Chambers, E. (2000). *Native Tours—The Anthropology of Travel and Tourism*. Prospect Heights, Ill., Waveland Press.

Cheong, S.-M., and Marc L. Miller (2000). Power and Tourism—A Foucauldian Observation. *Annals of Tourism Research* 27(2):371–390.

Clancy, M. J. (1999). "Tourism and Development—Evidence from Mexico." *Annals of Tourism Research* 26(1):1–20.

Cieply, M., and Claudia Eller (2003). Disney Film Remembers the Alamo, Inclusively. *Los Angeles Times*, February 24, A12.

Clark, J. (2003). Vacationing Large. Mexican Resort Offers Big Travelers a Just-My-Size Trip. *USA Today*, July 11, 1-2D.

Clottes, J., and C. Chippendale. (1999). The Parc Pyrénéen d'Art Prehistorique, France: Beyond Replica and Re-enactment in Interpreting the Ancient Past. In *Constructed Past, Experimental Archaeology, Education and the Public*, P. G. Stone, and Philippe G. Planel, eds., 194–205. London, Routledge.

Coe, A. (2001). *Archaeological Mexico: A Traveler's Guide to Ancient Cities and Sacred Sites*. Emeryville, Calif., Avalon Travel Publishing.

Coe, M. D. (1993). *The Maya*. London, Thames and Hudson.

Cohen, E. (1978). "The Impact of Tourism on the Physical Environment." *Annals of Tourism Research* 5:215–237.

Cone, C. A. (1995). "Crafting Selves: The Lives of Two Mayan Women." *Annals of Tourism Research* 22(2):314–327.

Cornelius, W. A., and David Myhre, eds. (1998). *The Transformation of Rural Mexico—Reforming the Eiido Sector*. Center for U.S.–Mexican Studies. La Jolla, University of San Diego.

Cothran, D. A., and Cheryl Cole Cothran (1998). "Promise or Political Risk for Mexican Tourism." *Annals of Tourism Research* 25(2):477–497.

Crick, M. (1989). "Representations of International Tourism in the Social Sciences: Sun, Sex, Sights, Savings, and Servility." *Annual Review of Anthropology* 18:307–344.

Daltabuit, M., and Thomas Leatherman (1998). The Biocultural Impact of Tourism on Mayan Communities. In *Building a New Biocultural Synthesis—Political-Economic Perspectives on Human Biology*, A. Goodman and T. Leatherman, eds., 317–337. Ann Arbor, University of Michigan Press.

Daltabuit, M., and Oriol Pi-Sunyer (1990). "Tourism Development in Quintana Roo, Mexico." *Cultural Survival Quarterly* 14(1): Part One, 9–13.

d'Arc, H. R. (1980). Change and Rural Emigration in Central Mexico. In *Environment, Society, and Rural Change in Latin America*, D. A. Preston, ed., 185–194. Chichester, John Wiley & Sons.

Davidson, T. L. (1994). What Are Travel and Tourism: Are They Really an Industry? In

Global Tourism in the Next Decade, W. F. Theobald, ed., 20–26. Oxford, Butterworth-Heinemann Ltd.

Davis, K. L. (1997). Sites without Sights: Interpretive Closed Excavations. In *Presenting Archaeology to the Public*, J. H. Jameson, Jr., ed., 84–98. Walnut Creek, Calif., Altamira Press.

Davis, P. (2000). Museums and the Promotion of Environmental Understanding and Heritage Conservation. In *Cultural Resource Management in Contemporary Society.* F. B. McManamon, and Alf Hatton, eds., 310–318. London, Routledge.

De Bloois, E. I., and Kent A. Schneider (1989). Cultural Resource Management in the USDA Forest Service. In *Archaeological Heritage Management in the Modern World*, H. Cleere, ed., 227–231. London, Unwin Hyman.

de Janvry, A., Gustavo Gordillo, and Elisabeth Sadoulet (1997). *Mexico's Second Agrarian Reform*. La Jolla, Ejido Reform Research Project Center for U.S.–Mexican Studies, University of California at San Diego.

de Kadt, E., ed. (1978). *Tourism, Passport to Development? Perspectives on the Social and Cultural Effects of Tourism in Developing Countries.* New York, Oxford University Press.

DeLoach, N. (1986). "The Ancient Caves of the Maya." *Ocean Realm* (Fall):64–71.

de Tapia, E. M. (2002). "A First Look at Public Outreach in Mexican and Guatemalan Archaeology." *The SAA Archaeological Record* 2(2):27–29.

DeVita, P. R. (2000). *Stumbling Toward Truth: Anthropologists at Work.* Prospect Heights, Ill., Waveland Press, Inc.

Dufresne, L. (1999). *Les Mayas et Cancún.* Montréal, Les Presses de L'Université de Montréal.

Dumond, D. E. (1977). Independent Maya of the Late Nineteenth Century: Chiefdoms and Power Politics. In *Anthropology and History in Yucatán*, G. D. Jones, ed., 103–138. Austin and London, University of Texas Press.

Dumond, D. E. (1997). *The Machete and the Cross: Campesino Rebellion in Yucatán.* Lincoln, University of Nebraska Press.

Fagan, Garret O. (2003). Far-Out Television. *Archaeology Magazine*, May–June.

Farriss, N. (1984). *Maya Society Under Colonial Rule: The Collective Enterprise of Survival.* Princeton, Princeton University Press.

Farriss, N., and Arthur O. Miller (1977). "Maritime Culture Contact of the Maya: Underwater Surveys and Test Excavations in Quintana Roo." *International Journal of Nautical Archaeology and Underwater Exploration* 6:141–151.

Faust, B. B. (2001). "Maya Environmental Successes and Failures in the Yucatán Peninsula." *Environmental Science and Policy* 4:153–169.

Fedick, S. L. (2003). In Search of the Maya Forest. In *In Search of the Rain Forest*, Candace Slater, ed. Durham, N.C., Duke University Press.

Fischer, E. F., and R. McKenna Brown, ed. (1996). *Maya Cultural Activism in Guatemala.* Austin, University of Texas Press.

FONATUR (n.d.). Cancún un Sueno Convertido en Realidad. Cancún.

FONATUR (1993). Panel Aeropuerto: Estudio Continuo de Visitantes Pro Via Aerea. Mexico City, FONATUR: Subdireccion General de Comercializacion.

Ford, A. (1999). Using the Past to Preserve the Future: Maya Ruins Are the Heart of a Bold Economic Plan. *Discovering Archaeology* September–October:98–101.

Friedland, J. (1999). "Paved Paradise: Build First, Ask Later." *Wall Street Journal,* A12.

Frost, N. R. (2000). Environmental Education: Perspectives for Archaeology. In *The Archaeology Education Handbook,* K. Smardz and S. J. Smith, eds., 377–393. Walnut Creek, Calif., Altamira Press.

Galletti, H. (1998). The Maya Forest of Quintana Roo, Mexico. In *Timber, Tourists and Temples,* R. Primack, David Bray, Hugo Galletti, and Ismael Ponciano, eds., 33–46. Washington, D.C., Island Press.

Gamio, M. (1960). *Forjando Patria: Pro-nacionalismo.* Mexico City, Porrua.

Garcia, R. (2000). "Maya Development Plan 85% Complete." *The Miami Herald,* August 14, 3A.

Garrett, Wilbur E. (1989). "La Ruta Maya." *National Geographic Magazine,* 176, no. 4 (October):424–506.

Getz, D. (1994). Event Tourism and the Authenticity Dilemma. In *Global Tourism—The Next Decade.* W. F. Theobald, ed., 313–329. Oxford, Butterworth-Heinemann Ltd.

Gifford, J. C. (1978). The Ancient Maya in Light of Their Ethnographic Present. In *Cultural Continuity in Mesoamerica,* D. L. Browman, ed., 205–228. The Hague, Mouton Publishers.

Goldin, L. R. (1999). Rural Guatemala in Economic and Social Transition. In *Globalization and the Rural Poor in Latin America.* W. M. Loker, ed., 93–110. Boulder and London, Lynne Rienner Publishers.

Gomez-Pompa, A., and A. Kaus (1998). "From Prehistoric to Future Conservation Alternatives: Lessons from Mexico." In *NAS Colloquium, Plants and Population: Is There Time?* Beckman Center of the National Academy of Sciences, University of California, Irvine.

Graburn, N. (1983). "The Anthropology of Tourism." *Annals of Tourism Research* 10(1): 9–33.

Greenwood, D. J. (1982). "Cultural 'Authenticity.'" *Cultural Survival Quarterly* 6(3): 27–28.

Greenwood, D. J. (1989). Culture by the Pound: An Anthropological Perspective on Tourism as Cultural Commoditization. In *Hosts and Guests: The Anthropology of Tourism,* V. L. Smith, ed., 171–185. Philadelphia, University of Pennsylvania Press.

Gregg, W., Jr., and B. A. McGean (1985). "Biosphere Reserves: Their History and Their Promise." *Orion* 4(3):40–51.

Gutiérrez, N. (1999). *Nationalist Myths and Ethnic Identities.* Lincoln and London, University of Nebraska Press.

Hale, C. R. (1997). "Cultural Politics of Identity in Latin America." *Annual Review of Anthropology* 26:567–590.

Halffter, G. (1980). "Biosphere Reserves and National Parks: Complementary Systems of Natural Protection." *Impact of Science on Society* 30(4):268–277.

Hardesty, D. L., and Barbara J. Little (2000). *Assessing Site Significance: A Guide for Archaeologists and Historians.* Walnut Creek, Calif., Altamira Press.

Harkin, M. (1995). "Modernist Anthropology and Tourism of the Authentic." *Annals of Tourism Research* 22(3):650–670.

Harris, R. (1999). *Hidden Cancún and the Yucatán*. Berkeley, Ulysses Press.

Hashimoto, A. (2000). "Being Ourselves to You: The Global Display of Cultures." *Annals of Tourism Research* 27(1):246–248.

Hawkins, D. E. (1994). Ecotourism: Opportunities for Developing Countries. In *Global Tourism in the Next Decade*, W. F. Theobald, ed., 261–273. Oxford, Butterworth Heinemann Ltd.

Hervik, P. (1994). Shared Reasoning in the Field: Reflexivity Beyond the Author. In *Social Experience and Anthropological Knowledge*, K. Hastrup and P. Hervik, eds., 78–100. London and New York, Routledge.

Hervik, P. (1999). *Mayan People Within and Beyond Boundaries*. Amsterdam, Harwood Academic Publishers.

Hillery, M., Blair Nancarrow, Graham Griffin, and Geoff Syme (2001). "Tourist Perception of Environmental Impact." *Annals of Tourism Research* 28(4):853–867.

Hobgood, J., and Carroll L. Riley (1978). Mesoamericans as Cultural Brokers in Northern New Spain. In *Cultural Continuity in Mesoamerica*, D. L. Browman, ed., 259–272. The Hague, Mouton Publishers.

Hollinshead, K. (1996). Marketing and Metaphysical Realism: The Disidentification of Aboriginal Life and Traditions Through Tourism. In *Tourism and Indigenous Peoples*, R. Butler and T. Hinch, ed., 308–348. London, International Thomson Business Press.

Honey, M. (1999). *Ecotourism and Sustainable Development: Who Owns Paradise?* Washington, D.C., Island Press.

Horne, D. (1984). *The Great Museum: The Representation of History*. London, Pluto Press.

Hostettler, U. (1997). Estratificacion Socioeconómica y Economia Domestica en el Municipio de Felipe Carrillo Puerto, Quintana Roo. *Persistencia Cultural Entre Los Mayas Frente Al Cambio y La Modernidad*, R. A. Mann and Ruth Gabler, eds., 17–40. Mérida, Universidad Autonoma de Yucatán.

Hostettler, U. (2001). Milpa, Land, and Identity: A Central Quintana Roo Mayan Community in a Historical Perspective. In *Maya Survivalism,* U. Hostettler and M. Restall, eds., 12: 239–262. Schwaben, Germany, Acta Mesoamericana.

Hostettler, U., ed. (1996). *Los Mayas de Quintana Roo Investigaciones Antropologicas Recientes*. Bern, Instituts fur Ethnologie der Universitat Bern.

Hostettler, U., and M. Restall., eds. (2001). *Maya Survivalism*. Schwaben, Germany, Acta Mesoamericana.

Howe, G. P. (1911). "The Ruins of Tuloom." *American Anthropologist* 13:539–550.

Howry, J. C. (1978). Ethnographic Realities of Mayan Prehistory. In *Cultural Continuity in Mesoamerica*, D. L. Browman, ed., 239–258. The Hague, Mouton Publishers.

Instituto National Indigenista Mexico (2002). Portal de Los Pueblos Indigenas. Programas y Proyectos del Instituto Nacional Indigenista—Dirección de Operation y Desarrollo, Electronic document, http://www.ini.gob.mx/ini/programas.html, accessed March 14, 2002.

Jameson, J. H., Jr., ed. (1997). *Presenting Archaeology to the Public*. Walnut Creek, Calif., Altamira Press.

Jameson, J. H., Jr. (2000). Public Interpretation, Education, and Outreach: The Growing Predominance in American Archaeology. In *Cultural Resource Management in Contemporary Society*, F. B. McManamon and Alf Hatton, eds., 288–299. London, Routledge.

Jameson, J. H., Jr., and William J. Hunt, Jr. (1999). Reconstruction Versus Preservation-in-Place in the U.S. National Park Service. In *The Constructed Past: Experimental Archaeology, Education and the Public*, P. G. Stone and P. G. Planel, eds., 35–61. London and New York, Routledge.

Johnston, B. (1990). "Introduction: Breaking Out of the Tourist Trap." *Cultural Survival Quarterly* 31(3):2–5.

Jones, G. D., ed. (1977). *Anthropology and History in Yucatán*. Austin and London, University of Texas Press.

Joseph, G. M. (1991). Introduction: The New Regional Historiography at Mexico's Periphery. In *Land, Labor, and Capital in Modern Yucatán: Essays in Regional History and Political Economy*, J. T. Brannon, and Gilbert M. Joseph, eds., 1-9. Tuscaloosa and London, The University of Alabama Press.

Juárez, A. M. (2002a). "Ecological Degradation, Global Tourism, and Inequality: Maya Interpretations of the Changing Environment in Quintana Roo, Mexico." *Human Organization* 61(2):113–124.

Juárez, A. M. (2002b). "Ongoing Struggles: Mayas and Immigrants in Tourist Era Tulum." *Journal of Latin American Anthropology* 7(1).

Kaplan, F. S. (1993). Mexican Museums in the Creation of a National Image in World Tourism. In *Crafts in the World Market*, J. Nash, ed., 103–126. Albany, State University of New York Press.

Kaus, A. (1992). "Common Ground: Ranchers and Researchers in the Mapimi Biosphere Reserve." *Anthropology*. Riverside, University of California.

Kelly, J. (1993). *An Archaeological Guide to Mexico's Yucatán Peninsula*. Norman and London, University of Oklahoma.

Kennedy, R. G. (2002). Foreword: The Value of Archaeology. In *Public Benefits of Archaeology*, B. J. Little, ed., xiii–xv. Gainesville, University Press of Florida.

Konrad, H. W. (1991). Capitalism on the Tropical-Forest Frontier: Quintana Roo, 1880s to 1930. In *Land, Labor, and Capital in Modern Yucatán: Essays in Regional History and Political Economy*, J. T. Brannon and Gilbert M. Joseph, eds., 143–171. Tuscaloosa and London, The University of Alabama Press.

Kwas, M. L. (2000). On Site and Open to the Public: Education at Archaeological Parks. In *The Archaeology Education Handbook*, K. Smardz and S. J. Smith, eds., 340–351. Walnut Creek, Calif., Altamira Press.

Kwas, M. L., and Robert C. Mainfort, Jr. (1996). "From Ancient Site to Tourist Attraction and Beyond." *Common Ground* 1(1):32–38.

León, L. V. (1994). Mexico: The Institutionalization of Archaeology, 1885–1942. In *History of Latin American Archaeology*, A. Oyuela-Caycedo, ed., 69–89. Aldershot and Brookfield, Avebury.

León-Portilla, M., ed. (1988). *Time and Reality in the Thought of the Maya*. Norman and London, University of Oklahoma Press.

Lerner, S., and Teresa Hoffman (2000). Bringing Archaeology to the Public: Programmes in the Southwestern United States. In *Cultural Resource Management in Contemporary Society: Perspectives on Managing and Presenting the Past*, F. B. McManamon, and Alf Hatton, eds., 231–246. London and New York, Routledge.

Lipe, W. (1984). Value and Meaning in Cultural Resources. In *Approaches to the Archaeological Record*, H. Cleere, ed., 1–11. Cambridge, Cambridge University Press.

Litvak, J. (1985). La Escuela Mexicana de Arqueologia: Un Desarrollo Científico Mexicano. Serie Los Nuestros–UNAM. Mexico.

Lockwood, J. M. (1989). *The Yucatán Peninsula*. Baton Rouge, Louisiana State University Press.

Los Angeles Times (2003a). Yucatán—Paradise in Peril. January 22.

Los Angeles Times (2003b). Zapatistas Seize a Tourist Ranch. March 1, A5. Lovell, W. G. (1990). "Maya Survival in Ixil Country, Guatemala." *Cultural Survival Quarterly* 14(4): 10–12.

Lynott, M. J., and Alison Wylie, eds. (2000). *Ethics in American Archaeology*. Washington, D.C., The Society for American Archaeology.

MacCannell, D. (1976). *The Tourist: A New Theory of the Leisure Class*. Berkeley and Los Angeles, University of California Press.

McClung de Tapia, E. (2002). "Exchanges: A First Look at Public Outreach in Mexican and Guatemalan Archaeology." *The SAA Archaeological Record* 2:27–29.

McManamon, F. B. (2000a). Public Education: A Part of Archaeological Professionalism. In *The Archaeology Education Handbook*, K. Smardz and S. J. Smith, eds., 17–24. Walnut Creek, New York, and London, Altamira Press.

McManamon, F. B. (2000b). The Protection of Archaeological Resources in the United States: Reconciling Preservation with Contemporary Society. In *Cultural Resource Management in Contemporary Society*, F. B. McManamon and Alf Hatton, eds., 40–54. London, Routledge.

McManamon, F. B., and Alf Hatton, eds. (2000). *Cultural Resource Management in Contemporary Society: Perspectives on Managing and Presenting the Past*. London and New York, Routledge.

Merriman, N. (2000). The Crisis of Representation in Archaeological Museums. In *Cultural Resource Management in Contemporary Society*, F. B. McManamon and Alf Hatton, eds., 300–309. London, Routledge.

Montague, B. (1997). Peso Crunch Attracts Cost-Conscious Tourists. *USA Today*, February 18, 10B.

Moreno, J., and Mary Ann Littrell (2001). "Negotiating Tradition—Tourism Retailers in Guatemala." *Annals of Tourism Research* 28(3):658–685.

Mowforth, M., and Ian Munt (1998). *Tourism and Sustainability: New Tourism in the Third World*. London and New York, Routledge.

Muriel, A. M. (2001). Archaeological Research in Mexico's Monumental Sites. In *Archaeological Research and Heritage Preservation in the Americas*, R. D. Drennan and Santiago Mora, eds., 56–62. Washington, D.C., The Society for American Archaeology.

Nash, D. (1989). Tourism as a Form of Imperialism. In *Hosts and Guests: The Anthropology of Tourism*, V. L. Smith, ed., 37–52. Philadelphia, University of Pennsylvania Press.

Nash, J. C. (2001). *Mayan Visions The Quest of Autonomy in an Age of Globalization.* New York and London, Routledge.

Nash, J. C., ed. (1993). *Crafts in the World Market.* Albany, State University of New York Press.

National Geographic (1989). La Ruta Maya. *National Geographic,* October 176(4): 424–506.

National Geographic (2003). A New Path to Maya Tourism. *National Geographic: Behind the Scenes,* August, n.p.

National Trust for Historic Preservation (2001). *Heritage Tourism Program.* National Trust for Historic Preservation, Washington, D.C.

Ness, S. A. (2003). *Where Asia Smiles.* Philadelphia, University of Pennsylvania Press.

New York Times (2001). Private Sector: The Marketer from Mexico. August 2, sec. 3, p. 2.

Ochoa, F. L. (1991). *Tourism Investment in Mexico.* San Diego, Institute for Regional Studies of the Californias, San Diego State University.

Oppenheimer, A. (1996). *Bordering on Chaos: Guerrillas, Stockbrokers, Politicians, and Mexico's Road to Prosperity.* Boston, Little, Brown and Co.

Oyuela-Caycedo, A. (1994). Nationalism and Archaeology: A Theoretical Perspective. In *History of Latin American Archaeology,* A. Oyuela-Caycedo, ed., 3–21. Aldershot and Brookfield, Avebury, U.K.

Oyuela-Caycedo, A., ed. (1994). *History of Latin American Archaeology.* Aldershot, Brookfield USA, Avebury.

Palerm, A. (1975), "La Disputa de los Antropologos Mexicanos Una Contribucion Cientifica." *America Indigena* 35 (January–March):161–177.

Parrent, J. M. (1988). Treasure Hunters in the Caribbean: The Current Crisis. In *Underwater Archaeology Proceedings from the Society for Historical Archaeology Conference.* Reno, Nevada, Society for Historical Archaeology.

Passariello, P. (1983). "Never on Sunday? Mexican Tourists at the Beach." *Annals of Tourism Research* 10:109–122.

Patch, R. W. (1991). Decolonization, the Agrarian Problem, and the Origins of the Caste War, 1812–1847. In *Land, Labor, and Capital in Modern Yucatán: Essays in Regional History and Political Economy,* J. T. Brannon and Gilbert M. Joseph, eds., 51–82. Tuscaloosa and London, The University of Alabama Press.

Pawlik, Chuck (2003). Near Cancún, Yet a World Away. *Los Angeles Times,* May 4, L11.

Paynton, C. (2002). "Public Perception and 'Pop' Archaeology: A Survey of Current Attitudes Toward Televised Archaeology in Britain." *The SAA Archaeological Record.* 2:33–36.

Pearce, K. (1984). *The View from the Top of the Temple: Ancient Maya Civilization and Modern Maya Culture.* Albuquerque, University of New Mexico Press.

Penalosa, F. (1996). *The Mayan Folktale: An Introduction.* Rancho Palos Verdes, Calif., Yax Te' Press.

Pfeiler, B. (1997). El Maya: Una Cuestión de Persistencia o Pérdida Cultural. In *Persistencia Cultural Entre Los Mayas Frente Al Cambio y La Modernidad,* R. A. Mann and Ruth Gamer, eds., 55–70. Mérida, Universidad Autonoma de Yucatan.

Pi-Sunyer, O., and R. Brooke Thomas (1997). Tourism, Environmentalism, and Cultural

Survival in Quintana Roo. In *Life and Death Matters*, B. Johnston, ed., 187–212. Walnut Creek and London, Altamira Press.

Pi-Sunyer, O., R. Brooke Thomas, and Magali Daltabuit (1999). "Tourism and Maya Society in Quintana Roo, Mexico." *Latin American Studies Consortium of New England*, Occasional Paper No. 17.

Pi-Sunyer, O., R. Brooke Thomas, and Magali Daltabuit (2001). Tourism on the Maya Periphery. In *Hosts and Guests Revisited: Tourism Issues of the 21st Century*, V. L Smith and Maryann Brent, eds., 122–140. New York, Cognizant Communication Corporation.

Potter, F. B., Jr. (1997). The Archaeological Site as an Interpretive Environment. In *Presenting Archaeology to the Public*, J. H. Jameson, Jr., ed., 35–44. Walnut Creek, Calif., Altamira Press.

Potter, F. B., Jr., and Mary Jo Chabot (1997). Locating Truths on Archaeological Sites. In *Presenting Archaeology to the Public*, J. H. Jameson, Jr., ed., 45–53. Walnut Creek, Calif., Altamira Press.

Press, I. (1977). Historical Dimensions of Orientation to Change in a Yucatec Peasant Community. In *Anthropology and History in Yucatán*, G. D. Jones, ed., 275–288. Austin and London, University of Texas Press.

Price, C. A. (2000). Following Fashion: The Ethics of Archaeological Conservation. In *Cultural Resource Management in Contemporary Society*, F. B. McManamon and Alf Hatton, eds., 213–230. London and New York, Routledge.

Primack, R., David Bray, Hugo Galletti, and Ismael Ponciano, eds. (1998). *Timber, Tourists, and Temples*. Washington, D.C., Island Press.

Pyburn, K. A., and Richard R. Wilk (2000). Responsible Archaeology Is Applied Archaeology. In *Ethics in American Archaeology*, M. J. Lynott and Alison Wylie, eds., 78–83. Washington, D.C., The Society for American Archaeology.

Rapley, J. (2002). *Understanding Development Theory and Practice in the Third World*. Boulder and London, Lynne Rienner Publishers.

Re Cruz, A. (1996). *The Two Milpas of Chan Kom*. Albany, State University of New York Press.

Redfield, R. (1950). *A Village That Chose Progress*. Chicago, The University of Chicago Press.

Redfield, R., and A. Villa Rojas (1962). *Chan Kom: A Maya Village*. Chicago, The University of Chicago Press.

Reed, N. A. (1964). *The Caste War of Yucatán*. Stanford, Stanford University Press.

Repetto, F. F., and Genny Negroe Sierra (1997). Resistencia Cultural a Través de Ia Religion Popular. Los Gremios y las Fiestas de Yucatán. In *Persistencia Cultural Entre Los Mayas Frente Al Cambio y La Modernidad*, R. A. Mann and Ruth Gabler, eds., 1–16. Mérida, Universidad Automa de Yucatán.

Restall, M. (1997). Persistencia Cultural Maya: La Evidencia de Documentos Notariales en el Yucatán Colonial. *Persistencia Cultural Entre Los Mayas Frente Al Cambio y La Modernidad*, R. A. Mann and Ruth Gabler, eds., 41–54. Mérida, Universidad Autonoma de Yucatán.

Riviera Maya Association of Dive and Watersport Operators (APSA) (2003). Cavern Guide Training Handbook. Published by the Riviera Maya APSA.

Robles Garcia, N. M. (2002). The Management of Archaeological Resources in Mexico:

Oaxaca as a Case Study. Electronic Document, Society for American Archaeology (accessed September 29, 2002).

Roys, R. L. (1957). *The Political Geography of the Yucatán Maya.* Publication 613. Washington, D.C., Carnegie Institution of Washington.

Rugeley, T. (1996). *Yucatán's Maya Peasantry and the Origins of the Caste War.* Austin, University of Texas Press.

Rugeley, T., ed. (2001). *Maya Wars: Ethnographic Accounts from Nineteenth-Century Yucatán.* Norman, University of Oklahoma Press.

Ryder, J. W. (1977). Internal Migration in Yucatán: Interpretation of Historical Demography and Current Patterns. In *Anthropology and History in Yucatán*, G. D. Jones, ed., 191–232. Austin and London, University of Texas Press.

Schavelzon, D. (1981). "Historia Social de la Restauración Arquitectonica en Mexico." *Vivenda* 6:434–477.

Schluter, R. G. (1994). Tourism Development: A Latin American Perspective. In *Tourism in the Next Decade*, W. F. Theobald, ed., 246–260. Oxford, Butterworth Heinemann, Ltd.

Schuster, A.M.H. (1999). "Faux Maya." *Archaeology Magazine*, January–February, 52:88.

SECTUR (1991). Mexico's Tourism Sector: The Year in Review. Mexico City, SECTUR.

SECTUR (1992). Estadisticas Bésicas de La Actividad Turistica. Mexico City, SECTUR.

Simonian, L. (1979). *Defending the Land of the Jaguar: A History of Conservation in Mexico.* Austin, University of Texas Press.

Slick, K. (2002). Archaeology and the Tourism Train. In *Public Benefits of Archaeology*, B. J. Little, ed., 219–227. Gainesville, University Press of Florida.

Smardz, K. E. (1997). The Past Through Tomorrow: Interpreting Toronto's Heritage to a Multicultural Public. In *Presenting Archaeology to the Public*, J. H. Jameson, Jr., ed., 101–113. Walnut Creek, Calif., Altamira Press.

Smith, M. E. (2001). Archaeology in the Middle of Political Conflict in Yautepec, Mexico. In *Working Together: Native Americans and Archaeologists*, K. E. Dongoske, Mark Aldenderfer, and Karen Doebner, eds., 191–197. Washington, D.C., The Society for American Archaeology.

Smith, V. L. (1996). Indigenous Tourism: The Four H's. In *Tourism and Indigenous Peoples*, R. Butler and T. Hinch, eds., 283–307. London, International Thomson Business Press.

Smith, V. L. (2001). Stone Age to Star Trek. In *Hosts and Guests Revisited: Tourism Issues of the 21st Century*, V. L. Smith and Mary Ann Brent, eds., 15–27. New York, Cognizant Communication Corporation.

Smith, V. L., ed. (1989). *Hosts and Guests: The Anthropology of Tourism.* Philadelphia, University of Pennsylvania Press.

Smith, V. L., and Mary Ann Brent (1978). *Hosts and Guests: The Anthropology of Tourism.* Oxford, Blackwell.

Smith, V. L., and Mary Ann Brent (2001). Introduction. In *Hosts and Guests Revisited: Tourism Issues of the 21st Century*, V. L. Smith and Mary Ann Brent, eds., 1–14. New York, Cognizant Communication Corporation.

Stephens, J. L. (1841). *Incidents of Travel in Central America, Chiapas, and Yucatan.* Reprinted 1962. New York, Harper.

Stephens, J. L. (1843). *Incidents of Travel in the Yucatán*. Reprinted 1996. Washington and London, Smithsonian Institution Press.

Stone, P. G. (1997). Presenting the Past: A Framework for Discussion. In *Presenting Archaeology to the Public*. J. H. Jameson, Jr., ed., 23–34. Walnut Creek, Calif., Altamira Press.

Stone, P. G., and Philippe G. Planel, eds. (1999). *The Constructed Past: Experimental Archaeology, Education and the Public*. London and New York, Routledge.

Stronza, A. (2001). "Anthropology of Tourism: Forging New Ground for Ecotourism and Other Alternatives." *Annual Review of Anthropology* 30:261–283.

Sullivan, P. (1983). Contemporary Yucatec Maya Apocalyptic Prophecy: The Ethnographic and Historical Context, Ph.D. dissertation, Johns Hopkins University.

Sullivan, P. (1989). *Unfinished Conversations: Mayas and Foreigners Between Two Wars*. New York, Alfred A. Knoff.

Sutherland, A. (1996). "Tourism and the Human Mosaic in Belize." *Urban Anthropology* 25(3):259–281.

Taube, K. (1993). *Aztec and Maya Myths*. Austin, British Museum Press and University of Texas Press.

Taube, K. (2001). Ancient and Contemporary Maya Conceptions of the Field and Forest. Paper presented at the 21st Symposium in Plant Biology, University of California, Riverside.

Thomas, D. H. (2002). Roadside Ruins: Does America Still Need Archaeology Museums? In *Public Benefits of Archaeology*, B. J. Little, ed., 130–145. Gainesville, University Press of Florida.

Thomas, J. (1996). *Time, Culture and Identity an Interpretive Archaeology*. London and New York, Routledge.

Thompson, E. H. (1992). The Sacred Well of the Itzaes. In *Artifacts from the Cenote of Sacrifice, Chichen Itza, Yucatán: Textiles, Basketry, Stone, Bone, Shell, Ceramics, Wood, Copal, Rubber, Other Organic Materials, and Mammalian Remains. Memoirs of the Peabody Museum of Archaeology and Ethnology*, C. C. Coggins, ed., 10:1–8. Cambridge, Harvard University Press.

Thurot, J. M., and Gaetane Thurot (1983). "The Ideology of Class and Tourism—Confining the Discourse of Advertising." *Annals of Tourism Research* 10:177–189.

Tozzer, A. M. (1957). *Chichén Itzá and Its Cenote of Sacrifice: A Comparative Study of Contemporaneous Maya and Toltec*. Cambridge, Mass., Harvard University Press.

Travel Channel (2003). "Top Ten Things to Do in Cancún." Televised, February 2003.

Travel Weekly (2001). Carnival Corp. to Build Cruise Port in Cancún. (Mexico). Electronic Document (November 15, 2001).

Trigger, B. G. (1984). "Alternative Archaeologists: Nationalist, Colonialist, Imperialist." *Man* 19 (n.s.): 355–370.

Tufts, S., and Simon Milne (1999). "Museums: A Supply-Side Perspective." *Annals of Tourism Research* 26(3):613–631.

Twain, M. (1869). *The Innocents Abroad, or, The New Pilgrim's Progress: being some account of the Steamship Quaker City's pleasure excursion to Europe and the Holy Land: with descriptions of countries, nations, incidents, and adventures, as they appeared to the author*. Hartford, Conn., American Publishing Co.

UzzelI, D., ed. (1989). *The Hot Interpretation of War and Conflict, Heritage Interpretation.* London, Belhaven Press.

van den Berghe, P. L. (1994). *The Quest for the Other.* Seattle and London, University of Washington Press.

van den Berghe, P. L. (1995). "Marketing Mayas Ethnic Tourism Promotion in Mexico." *Annals of Tourism Research* 22(3):568–599.

Vergano, D. (2001). Tourists Dig Expeditions Sponsored by Scientists. *USA Today*, Health & Science Section, August 21.

Viliesid, L., Ed. (1990). Quintana Roo I. Textos de su Historia. Dr. José Maria Mora, ed. San Juan Mixcoac, Mexico, Instituto de Investigaciones.

Villalobos Gonzalez, M. H. (1996). Mayas e Ingleses, Intercambio Economico aI Final de Ia Guerra de Castas 1880–1910. In *Los Mayas de Quintana Roo,* U. Hostettler, ed. Bern, Instituts fur Ethnologie der Universitat Bern.

Villalpando, M. E. (2001). Research, Conservation, and Rescuing Regional Identity in the Archaeology of Northwestern Mexico. In *Archaeological Research and Heritage Preservation in the Americas,* R. D. Drennan and Santiago Mora, eds., 49–55. Washington, D.C., The Society for American Archaeology.

Villa Rojas, A. (1945). *The Maya of East Central Quintana Roo.* Carnegie Institute of Washington, Publication 559. Washington, D.C.

Villa Rojas, A. (1962). "Notas sobre las distribucion y estado actual de la poblacion indigena de la peninsula de Yucatán, Mexico." *America Indigena* 22(3):209–240.

Villa Rojas, A. (1977). "El Proceso de Integracion Nacional Entre Los Mayas de Quintana Roo." *America Indigena* 37(4):883–905.

Villa Rojas, A. (1988). The Concept of Space and Time Among the Contemporary Maya. In *Time and Reality in the Thought of the Maya,* M. Leon Portilla, ed., 113–159. Norman and London, University of Oklahoma Press.

Waldren, J. (1997). We Are Not Tourists—We Live Here. In *Tourists and Tourism: Identifying with People and Places,* S. Abram, Jacqueline Waldren, and Donald V. L. Macleod, eds., 51–70. Oxford, Berg.

Wallerstein, I. (1974). *The Modern World-System.* New York, Academic Press.

Watanabe, J. M. (1995). "Unimagining the Maya: Anthropologists, Others, and the Inescapable Hubris of Authorship." *Bulletin of Latin American Research* 14(1):25–45.

Weaver, D. B. (1997). *Ecotourism in the Less Developed World.* Oxon, CAB International.

Weinbaum, B. (1997). "Disney Mediated Images Emerging in Cross-Cultural Expression on Isla Mujeres, Mexico." *Journal of American Culture* 20(2):19–36.

Williams, C. J. (2003). An Ugly Fight at Pretty Site: Developers Join Environmentalists to Oppose a Cruise-ship Pier on Mexico's Great Maya Reef. A Glut of Tourists Endangers the Area. *Los Angeles Times,* January 20.

World Tourism Organizanization (2000). *Market Research and Promotion, International Tourism Arrivals by Region.* Americas, World Tourism Organization.

Young, P. A. (2002). The Archaeologist as Storyteller. In *Public Benefits of Archaeology*, B. J. Little, ed., 239–243. Gainesville, University Press of Florida.

Index